THE GIFT OF FORGIVENESS

THE GIFT OF FORGIVENESS

CHARLES STANLEY

OLIVER
NELSON
™

THOMAS NELSON PUBLISHERS®
Nashville

A Division of Thomas Nelson, Inc.
www.ThomasNelson.com

Published in Nashville, Tennessee, by Thomas Nelson, Inc.

Unless otherwise noted, all Scripture quotations are taken from the NEW AMERICAN STANDARD BIBLE, copyright © The Lockman Foundation 1960, 1962, 1963, 1968, 1971, 1972, 1973, 1975, 1977, and are used by permission.

Scripture quotations noted NIV are from the HOLY BIBLE: NEW INTERNATIONAL VERSION. Copyright © 1973, 1978, 1984 by the International Bible Society. Used by permission of Zondervan.

Scripture quotations noted NKJV are from THE NEW KING JAMES VERSION. Copyright © 1979, 1980, 1982, Thomas Nelson, Inc. Publishers.

ISBN 0-7852-6415-9

Printed in the United States of America

03 04 05 06 PHX 5 4 3

CONTENTS

Preface

Forgiveness is a pivotal issue in the Christian walk, and *The Gift of Forgiveness* is just one of the books in the newly revised Charles Stanley Discipleship Series. Other books include *Eternal Security*, *How to Handle Adversity*, *Winning the War Within*, and *How to Listen to God*. This special series was created to support the building of a biblical foundation of faith and to lead to greater spiritual maturity. We encourage you to use these books as Bible study and witnessing tools.

When you have completed the Discipleship Series, we have more good news for you. In Touch Ministries has more on-going study for you on-line. We would like to invite you to explore our Web site at www.intouch.org. The pages of our site are filled with inspiration and exciting Bible study tools for the whole family. Take time today to browse the pages of our topical Scripture index, learn more about the heroes of the Bible in our Mighty in Spirit feature, or begin your quiet time with our daily on-line devotions. Also visit our Prayer Touch pages containing quick reference tips on prayer, quiet time aids for praying the Scriptures, and our monthly prayer-focused newsletter.

Children of all ages can grow in godliness with the tools in "Generation Next"—an area containing "Kids Corner" Bible lessons and printable activity pages, and "Teen Connection" age-specific Bible studies and encouraging daily devotions. This portion of the site also hosts "Parents Café," a priceless resource of godly inspiration for moms and dads.

May God bless you as you seek to grow in the disciplines of His Word and to pursue the goal of Christlike character.

—In Touch Ministries

In Touch Ministries is the teaching ministry of Dr. Charles F. Stanley, pastor of the 15,000-member First Baptist Church of Atlanta, Georgia. In Touch currently has a staff of more than 200 people in the United States and numerous affiliate staff throughout its international offices.

The real story of In Touch, however, is not statistical. It is the story of penetrating the human soul with the Word of God so that all who view or listen can grow to spiritual maturity and make a godly impact on the world in which they live.

Introduction

It was Sunday morning. As I drove toward the church, I rehearsed in my mind the events of the past months. I had been filling the pulpit as an associate pastor at the First Baptist Church of Atlanta while a committee searched high and low for a senior pastor to replace the man who had resigned. It was not long until the people began taking sides. One group wanted me as the pastor; another group wanted an older, more experienced, more well-known man. I was caught in the middle. My responsibility was simply to preach while the congregation battled it out among themselves.

The internal struggle that ensued left my family and me emotionally drained. I had been asked to leave on several occasions, and I would have been glad to go except for one reason: God said, "Stay." As my wife, Anna, and I prayed, we knew God was making it clear that we were to trust Him and remain where we were.

Now, after twelve months, it appeared that the end was in sight. In a very turbulent business meeting that lasted three hours, I had been elected the pastor of the church. It seemed as if we had hurdled all the major obstacles. Little did I know, however, that the greatest obstacle—the obstacle of forgiveness—was yet to come.

The following pages flow from my struggle to forgive people whom I trusted and loved as my friends, yet they proved otherwise. More than anything, this book is simply an invitation to deal with the poison of an unforgiving spirit. It is a poison capable of ruining not only your life, but the lives of those around you as well. It is my prayer that in these pages you will discover the freedom that comes from putting behind you once and for all the hurts and injustices of yesterday.

One

FORGIVENESS AND FREEDOM

Forgive him? Are you kidding? After what he has done to me? I can *never* forgive him!"

"Forgive me? How could God forgive me? You don't know what I have done."

"How could I have done such an awful thing? I can never forgive myself."

These are the confessions I hear every day as a pastor. Confessions from people who have grown up in churches, grown up with godly parents, and yet grown up without ever fully understanding God's forgiveness and its intended effect on every level of their lives.

The tragedy of all this is the bondage people find themselves in when they do not grasp the immensity of God's forgiveness. It is a bondage that stifles their ability to love and accept those they know in their hearts most deserve their love. It is a bondage that cripples marriages from their outset. It is a bondage that is often passed from generation to generation.

It is a bondage that chokes out the abundant life Christ promised to those who would believe.

That is why I felt compelled to write this book on forgiveness. Only by truly understanding God's forgiveness and making it a part of their lives will people be delivered from this bondage. Only then will they be able to enjoy the freedom that ensues and be able to live the Christian life to its fullest.

WHAT IS FORGIVENESS?

Forgiveness is "the act of setting someone free from an obligation to you that is a result of a wrong done against you." For example, a debt is forgiven when you free your debtor of his obligation to pay back what he owes you.

Forgiveness, then, involves three elements: *injury*, a *debt* resulting from the injury, and a *cancellation of the debt*. All three elements are essential if forgiveness is to take place. Before we look in more detail at this process, however, we need to trace the sequence of events that lead to bondage when this process is abandoned. This is important because I believe most people who suffer from an unforgiving spirit do not know that unforgiveness is the root of their problem.

All they know is that they just "can't stand" to be around certain people. They find themselves wanting to strike out at people when certain subjects are discussed. They feel uncomfortable around certain personality types. They lose their temper over little things. They constantly struggle with guilt over sins committed in the past. They can't get away from the ambivalence of hating the ones they know they should love the most. Such feelings and behavior patterns often indicate that people have not come to grips with the forgiveness of God and the implications of that forgiveness.

TAKING HOSTAGES

We are all painfully aware of what it means for somebody to be taken hostage. We are outraged when the news of such an atrocity reaches us. And yet when we refuse to forgive others (or ourselves, for that matter), there is a sense in which we hold them hostage. Let me explain.

When a person is taken hostage on the international scene, the abductors usually want something; it may be money, weapons, or the release of prisoners. The message they send, in essence is, "If you give us what we want, we will give you back what we have taken." There is always some type of condition, a ransom of some sort.

When individuals refuse to forgive others for a wrong done to them, they are saying the same thing. But instead of holding people hostage until they get their demands, they withhold love, acceptance, respect, service, kindness, patience, or whatever the others value. The message they send is this: "Until I feel you have repaid me for the wrong done to me, you will not have my acceptance." If we go back to our definition, we can see that the element missing from this scenario is *cancellation of the debt*. Persons who refuse to forgive refuse to cancel the debt.

THE REAL LOSER

A person who has an unforgiving spirit is always the real loser, much more so than the one against whom the grudge is held. This is easy to see when we take a closer look at the things most people withhold from those they feel have wronged them. Unforgiveness, by its very nature, prevents individuals from following through on many of the specifics of the Christian life and practically necessitates that they walk by the flesh rather than by the Spirit.

Think about your own experience for a moment. Think back to the last time someone really hurt you or wronged you or took something that belonged to you, whether it was a possession or an opportunity.

Immediately following the incident, did you feel like running out and doing something kind for the person, or did you feel like retaliating? Did you consider responding in gentleness, or did you think about letting loose with some well-chosen words? Did you feel like giving in and accepting the situation, or did you feel like fighting for your "rights"?

If you were honest, you probably identified more with the latter option in each case. These are the normal responses to being hurt or taken advantage of. But think of these responses in light of what Paul says, and you will begin to understand why an improper response to injury automatically impairs a person's walk with God.

> But the fruit of the Spirit is love, joy, peace, patience, kindness, goodness, faithfulness, gentleness, self-control; against such things there is no law . . . If we live by the Spirit, let us also walk by the Spirit. (Gal. 5:22–23, 25)

In a broad sense Paul's list here includes all the things we naturally want to hold hostage from the people who have hurt us. We rarely want to give our love to individuals who have hurt us. We certainly have no joy or peace when others have injured us in some way. We are not generally patient with or kind to people who have wronged us. We could go right down the list.

Paul accurately describes the responses of the unforgiving person:

Now the deeds of the flesh are evident, which are . . . enmities, strife, jealousy, outbursts of anger, disputes, dissensions, factions, envying, . . . and things like these, of which I forewarn you just as I have forewarned you that those who practice such things shall not inherit the kingdom of God. (Gal. 5:19–21)

An unforgiving spirit prevents a person from being able to walk consistently in the Spirit. The only choice is to walk according to the flesh. The consequences of such a life are devastating, and Paul discusses what will happen:

Do not be deceived, God is not mocked: for whatever a man sows, this he will also reap. For the one who sows to his own flesh shall from the flesh reap *corruption*, but the one who sows to the Spirit shall from the Spirit reap eternal life. (Gal. 6:7–8, emphasis mine)

The corruption Paul mentions has nothing to do with hell. He is talking about the consequences on this earth. If a person—believer or nonbeliever—makes decisions according to the impulses and desires of the flesh, the result will always be corruption—a wrecked and ruined life. Those persons who have not come to grips with the concept of forgiveness have by the very nature of unforgiveness set themselves up to walk according to the flesh. When that happens, they are losers every time. By withholding patience, kindness, gentleness, self-control, and the rest, the individual is held hostage by the flesh and, thus, is the ultimate loser.

A CONSUMING CORRUPTION

The destructive nature of an unforgiving spirit is such that it is not limited to one relationship. Resentment and other negative feelings spill over into other relationships. This is the second reason a person with an unforgiving spirit loses out in life.

Unfortunately, people are rarely aware when hostility from one relationship affects their ability to get along with others. So they try and try—unsuccessfully—to work out their differences with others, never recognizing the real source of the problem. Once they tire of trying to change, they excuse their insensitivity as part of their personality and expect people to "work around" them, emotionally speaking. They develop a take-me-or-leave-me-but-don't-try-to-change-me attitude, and in the process they hurt people they love the most.

I see this spillover most often in marital relationships. When a husband and a wife come in for marriage counseling, I begin by asking about their relationships with their parents. Almost without fail, one of them feels some bitterness or resentment toward a parent (or parents). Sometimes both of them have these feelings. Oftentimes the root of their marriage problems is found in some hostility they have been hauling around, sometimes since childhood.

In almost every case, the counselees have a legitimate complaint—they have really been wronged by their parents. But their inability or unwillingness to forgive ends up hurting them, not their parents!

THE REJECTION CONNECTION

The third reason a person with an unforgiving spirit loses out in life is closely tied to the other reasons we've just discussed. When a person is wronged in some way, whether in marriage, business, friendship, or some other relationship, rejection occurs. The classic case would be when a guy breaks up with his girlfriend because he has found another girl. In her struggle with rejection the girl swears she will never trust another male.

It is easy to see where hurt resulted from rejection. But if we plug this concept into other sets of circumstances, we can see it holds true in every case where forgiveness is needed. The following incident, which set my son and me at odds for years, illustrates how an unforgiving spirit has feelings of rejection at its roots.

When Andy was about fourteen, he discovered he had some musical talents. He began spending a great deal of time playing the piano, primarily by ear. That meant a great deal of pounding chords with very little melody. To me, it sounded all the same.

One day on my way upstairs I stuck my head in the living room and said, "Andy, is that all you know?" To my uninformed ear, it sounded as if he had been playing the same song for hours! He immediately stopped playing. And he never played for me again. He would wait until my wife and I would leave the house, and then he would spend hours practicing and practicing. I began hearing from others what a fine pianist Andy was, but I never heard another sound from the piano in the living room.

Some years later—when Andy was in his twenties—our conversation turned toward his music. He gave me his version of what happened in the living room that afternoon, and he confessed that he had resented me from that day on. Why? It really was not a big deal to me. I did not mean anything serious by what I said. But to Andy, as a teenager, what I communicated was this: "I do not accept you or your music."

He was too young to understand that my comment was directed at his music, not at *him* as my son. And I was too insensitive to understand that the budding young artist saw little distinction between his work and his personhood. And so I crushed him; and he held it against me. By Andy's own admission, the resentment he held in his heart toward me spilled over into other relationships in his life, primarily those having to do with authority.

What I want you to understand is that the cause of his resentment was perceived rejection. I say "perceived" because I did not intend to reject him. His response, however, was the same as if it had been intentional.

Lost and Found

After years of listening to people recount how they have been hurt and mistreated by parents, spouses, kids, employers, and even pastors, I am convinced that at the beginning of each story is an experience that has been interpreted as rejection. As the rejection evolves into an unforgiving spirit, and eventually into bitterness, it takes a terrible toll. The person is left with a deep sense of emptiness, an inner sense that something is missing. Consequently, the individual seeks to regain what has been lost—and almost always in the context of relationships that are unrelated. Let me give an example to illustrate.

A counselor I know told me the following story. He said a father brought his daughter in for counseling after the father learned she had recently had an abortion. As the father began conveying his concern about the spiritual welfare of his daughter, it became apparent to my friend that the girl deeply resented her father. It was also clear that the daughter felt no remorse about what she had done, and she frankly did not want to be there.

She paid no attention to anything being said until the counselor began to explain the usual sequence of events that leads a young girl to become sexually active. Then he described what a father-daughter relationship should be like: how a father should spend time with his daughter, how he should show her proper affection and praise her for her character and accomplishments. He explained that when a father loves his daughter, she does not feel compelled to look for love the way his daughter had.

Before he could finish what he was saying, the girl interrupted. Looking at her father, she said, "You never loved me that way! You never spent time with me! You never listened to anything I had to say!"

Then to the shock of my friend, she turned to him and said, "I have never had love the way you described it, but I am willing to give anything to get it." As she spoke, she slowly slid her skirt up several inches.

An extreme example? Maybe, but not unrealistic. Some people will go to almost any extreme to find what they have lost through intentional or unintentional rejection. People harboring unresolved resentment can feel driven to explore all kinds of avenues—usually ones that are not in keeping with the Christian life.

THE WAITING GAME

There is a fourth reason an unforgiving spirit can devastate a life. Since the person with the unforgiving spirit is usually waiting for the other person to make restitution, a great deal of time may go by. During this time, fleshly patterns of behavior and incorrect thought processes develop. As I mentioned before, other relationships are damaged. Even after an unforgiving spirit is corrected, the side effects can take years to deal with, especially in the area of relationships.

The irony of the situation is this: By refusing to forgive and by waiting for restitution to be made, individuals allow their personal growth and development to hinge on the decision of others they dislike to begin with. They allow themselves to be held hostage. They say, "If he apologizes." "If she comes back to me." "If he rehires me." "If they invite me." They play the game of waiting for others to make the first move. In the meantime they allow an unforgiving spirit to weave its way into the total fabric of their lives.

Another ironic element is that sometimes the person who has done the wrong has no idea anything is wrong. A senior in the high-school department of our church had a good relationship with my son, who was serving as youth pastor at the time. Andy began to notice that Kim was not as friendly as she had been and that she became less and less involved in the youth department. He would make a point to speak to her, but his kindness was rarely returned.

After several months went by, he took the youths skiing. It so happened that late one evening on the trip Kim approached Andy and said she needed to talk. She began by apologizing for her attitude. She admitted she had been hurt by Andy and she had been holding something he said to her against him for some time. Then she asked him if he knew what he had said that hurt her so badly. Andy thought and thought and came up with nothing.

She looked surprised, reprimanded him for his insensitivity, and said, "Several months ago, I spoke to you in Sunday school and told you our family had just bought a new pet."

Andy still drew a blank.

She continued, "You asked me what we got, and I told you it was a bird. Do you remember what you said then?"

At that point Andy remembered the conversation as well as his response to the news that her family had acquired a bird.

"Yes," he said, "I do remember. I told you birds were messy and asked why you didn't get something more useful like a dog."

Andy immediately apologized, and his friendship with Kim was restored. Unfortunately, months were wasted because she would not deal with her hurt, and he did not know he had done anything.

A great deal of the hurt and rejection we face is unintentional. The seeming lack of concern on the part of those who hurt us is often not an attempt on their part to be insensitive.

SOME CHOOSE TO LOSE

From what we've examined in this chapter, I hope you clearly understand this: *A person who harbors unforgiveness always loses.* Regardless of how wrong the other person may have been, refusing to forgive means reaping corruption in life. And that corruption begins in one relationship, including the relationship with God, and works its way into all the rest.

Holding on to hurt is like grabbing a rattlesnake by the tail; you are going to be bitten. As the poison of bitterness works its way through the many facets of your personality, death will occur—death that is more far-reaching than your physical death, for it has the potential to destroy those around you as well.

MAKING THE PLUNGE

Have you been hurt? Has somebody, somewhere in your past, rejected you in such a way that you still hurt when you think about it? Do you become critical of people in your past the minute their names are mentioned? Did you leave home as a child or a college student with great relief that you were leaving, swearing you would never return?

Have you worked hard all your life not to become like your parents? Are there people in your past upon whom you would enjoy taking revenge? Have you made a pastime out of scheming about how you could get back at them or embarrass them publicly? Were you abused as a child? Maybe even molested? Did you suffer through your parents' divorce as a child? Were your parents taken from you when you were very young?

Were you forced by circumstances to pursue a different career from the one you originally wanted to pursue? Were you unable to attend the school of your choice because of financial reasons? Were you pushed out of a job opportunity by a greedy friend? Were you promised things by your employer that never came about?

If you answered yes to any of these questions, you may be on the brink of being set free from a bondage that you did not even know was keeping you a victim. You may be about to understand for the first time why you act the way you do in certain circumstances and why you cannot seem to control your temper. You may be on the verge of receiving the God-given insight you need to restore your war-torn home—this time for good.

Whatever your situation, whatever has happened in your past, remember that you are the loser if you do not deal with an unforgiving spirit. And the people around you suffer too.

I am writing so that you may be set free. In the process you may experience some pain. In some instances, it may be pain you have worked for years to avoid. Yet that pain is necessary for healing to take place.

It is my prayer that you will read each chapter carefully and prayerfully. It is my goal to bring old truths to bear on the damaging experiences of your life. And in doing so, I hope to give the Holy Spirit an opportunity to make you whole.

QUESTIONS FOR PERSONAL GROWTH

1. What does the word *forgiveness* mean?
2. What are the three essential elements of forgiveness?
3. Name four reasons why the person with an unforgiving spirit is the real loser.
4. What insights have you gained with regard to your past circumstances and your present actions?

Two

THE BIG PICTURE

Attitudes are difficult things to change. I can remember as a child being told to "change my attitude," as if there were some button I could push that would instantly cause something to happen inside my head! In dealing with an unforgiving spirit—or a grudge as some call it—people need a big change in attitude. The following story illustrates how attitudes may actually be changed.

Once there was a boy who lived with his mother and grandfather. His grandfather was not really an elderly man, but he was confined to a wheelchair and had very little use of his arms. His face was badly scarred, and he had a difficult time swallowing his food.

Every day the little boy was assigned the task of going into his grandfather's room and feeding him lunch. This the little boy did faithfully, but not joyously. It was quite a mess to feed Grandfather.

As the boy grew into adolescence, he became weary of his responsibility. One day he stormed into the kitchen and announced that he had had enough. He told his mother, "From now on, you can feed Grandfather."

Very patiently his mother turned from her chores, motioned for her son to sit down, and said, "You are a young man now. It is time you knew the whole truth about your grandfather." She continued, "Grandfather has not always been confined to a wheelchair. In fact he used to be quite an athlete. When you were a baby, however, there was an accident."

The boy leaned forward in his chair as his mother began to cry.

She said, "There was a fire. Your father was working in the basement, and he thought you were upstairs with me. I thought he was downstairs with you. We both rushed out of the house leaving you alone upstairs. Your grandfather was visiting at the time. He was the first to realize what happened. Without a word he went back into the house, found you, wrapped you in a wet blanket, and made a mad dash through the flames. He brought you safely to your father and me."

By this time the boy had tears in his eyes as well. He never knew; his grandfather never told him. And with no conscious effort on his part, *his attitude changed*. With no further complaints, he picked up his grandfather's lunch tray and took it to his room.

"NOW I SEE . . ."

Attitudes change when we get all the facts, when we see the big picture. In this chapter and the one that follows it we will be taking a look at the big picture concerning forgiveness. We will be gathering facts that will give us the perspective we need to understand the basis of God's forgiveness.

WHERE IT ALL BEGAN

Sin creates a deficit in God's economy. Whenever there is sin, something is taken or demanded from the sinner. In Genesis 3 the serpent lost its standing in the animal kingdom because of its part in the temptation of Adam and Eve (v. 14). Adam and Eve lost the perfect harmony that once characterized their relationship (v. 16). Adam and Eve lost their home in the Garden of Eden (v. 24). Chapter 4 of Genesis records that Cain lost his ability to effectively cultivate the ground. He also lost his place among men (vv. 12–14).

We could go right through the Scriptures illustrating this principle. Whenever there is sin, the sinner loses something that is outside the sinner's power to regain.

Another principle, however, runs parallel with this one. Historically, whenever human beings sin against God, He provides a channel through which fellowship can be reestablished and maintained. This is an important concept as we look into the idea of forgiveness because we see in it God's desire to have fellowship with sinful, disobedient men and women.

This principle demonstrates God's willingness to give the human race a second chance. As we look closer at this second principle, we will see that all of history is the outworking of God's strategy to bring humankind back into fellowship. The groundwork for your forgiveness and mine was laid immediately after the first sin was committed, and God has been building on that foundation ever since. The first clear example of this principle is in the case of Cain and Abel.

So it came about in the course of time that Cain brought an offering to the LORD of the fruit of the ground. And Abel, on his part also brought of the firstlings of his flock and of their fat portions.

And the LORD had regard for Abel and for his offering; but for Cain and for his offering He had no regard. (Gen. 4:3–5)

The Bible does not give us all the details surrounding this narrative, but some things are clear by way of implication. First, both Cain and Abel knew that they were to bring an offering to the Lord. Second, there was a distinction between a *proper* offering and an *improper* offering. Third, Cain and Abel knew what God considered proper and improper offerings. This is evident from God's response to Cain when He said, "If you do what is right, will you not be accepted?" (4:7 NIV).

This narrative is important to our discussion because it illustrates God's desire to have fellowship with members of the human race. The implication of the text is that immediately after the Fall, God instituted a way through which His people could restore fellowship with Him. God had every right in the world, humanly speaking, to break off His relationship with humankind after Adam and Eve sinned in the Garden. But God's love for us is so strong He delayed His wrath to give us a second chance.

LOOKING AHEAD

Another Old Testament example of God's desire to have fellowship with men and women is found in the sacrificial system as practiced in Israel. The book of Leviticus describes in detail the procedure an individual had to go through to maintain fellowship with God. To us, it seems complex; it looks as though God went out of His way to make it difficult for His people to get to Him. But the whole sacrificial system is actually a picture of God's grace because He provided a way for His people to get to Him.

Here is a brief overview of how the sacrificial system worked:

Then the LORD called to Moses and spoke to him from the tent of meeting, saying, "Speak to the sons of Israel and say to them, 'When any man of you brings an offering to the LORD, you shall bring your offering of animals from the herd or the flock. If his offering is a burnt offering from the herd, he shall offer it, a male without defect; he shall offer it at the doorway of the tent of meeting, that he may be accepted before the LORD. And he shall lay his hand on the head of the burnt offering, that it may be accepted for him to make atonement on his behalf.'" (Lev. 1:1–4)

The sacrificial system was a reminder that the penalty for sin is death. Instead of the sinner being put to death, however, an animal was put to death. To signify that the animal was the substitute, the person offering the sacrifice placed a hand on the head of the animal. As a result, the person was accepted before the Lord. The term *accepted* denotes fellowship with Him.

The system was God's way of allowing sinful men and women to carry on a relationship with the sinless Creator. God was under no obligation to provide such a system. Yet His desire for fellowship with His people was so strong He willingly went the extra mile to make such fellowship possible.

THE COVER-UP

The Old Testament uses an interesting word in connection with the forgiveness of God. That word is *atonement*. In Leviticus 6 we read:

And as a penalty he must bring to the priest, that is, to the LORD, his guilt offering, a ram from the flock, one without defect and of the proper value. In this way the priest will make atonement for him before the LORD, and he will be forgiven for any of these things he did that made him guilty. (Lev. 6:6–7 NIV)

Atonement means "to cover." It is the same Hebrew word translated "coat" in Genesis where God instructs Noah in how to build the ark: "So make yourself an ark of cypress wood; make rooms in it and coat it with pitch inside and out" (Gen. 6:14 NIV).

The significance of this term is that the sacrificial system was adequate for the time being, but it was temporary in nature. The sins of those living under the Levitical system were *covered* for the time, but not *forgiven* in the absolute sense of the word. Why not? Because the blood of animals cannot be sufficient payment for the debt incurred by sinners. The testimony of the New Testament affirms that fact:

But those sacrifices are an annual reminder of sins, because it is impossible for the blood of bulls and goats to take away sins. (Heb. 10:3–4 NIV)

At the beginning of this chapter I said that sin creates a deficit in God's economy. Whenever there is sin, something is taken or demanded from the sinner. What God ultimately requires of the sinner as a result of the sin is death—the death of the sinner. This is clear from God's warning to Adam in the Garden:

And the LORD God commanded the man, saying, "From any tree of the garden you may eat freely; but from the tree of the knowledge of good and evil you shall not eat, for in the day that you eat from it you shall surely die." (Gen. 2:16–17)

Paul confirms this:

Therefore, just as through one man sin entered into the world, and death through sin, and so death spread to all men, because all sinned. (Rom. 5:12)

As we study further in Scripture, we find that this death entails more than the giving up of physical life. It means eternal separation from God:

And if anyone's name was not found written in the book of life, he was thrown into the lake of fire. (Rev. 20:15)

WHAT'S THE HOLDUP?

So some questions arise: If the penalty for sin is death, why did God not immediately snuff out the lives of Adam and Eve? Did He not say that on the "day" they sinned they would "surely die"? Why does He not do the same for all sinners? What is He waiting for? Why did He provide Cain and Abel and later Israel with a system through which fellowship could be restored if sin ultimately resulted in death?

The answer is simple yet life-changing in its profundity. There is something God wants more than retribution. There is something He desires more than simply being paid back for the disrespect shown Him. God wants fellowship with us. And He was willing to put His own system of justice on hold while He made provision for sinful men and women to be rescued.

Notice I did not say God "bypassed" His system of justice.

He could not do that, because the system by which He abides is an expression of His very nature. What He did, as we have seen, was to come up with a temporary system through which His own righteous standards could be served.

IS THERE ANY DOUBT?

Before we go on, consider this crucial question: Do you realize that the God of the universe desires to have fellowship with you? You may say, "But you don't know what I've done!" I know this. Whatever you have done pales into insignificance beside the sin of Adam and Eve. They brought sin into the human race (Rom. 5:12). Their sin brought about God's curse on the whole earth (Gen. 3:17). Their sin made death a reality for all that breathes, both human and animal.

Yet after all that, God still cared enough about Adam and Eve to slay an animal and make garments of skin to cover their nakedness and hide their shame (Gen. 3:21). Although their sin was not taken away, it was covered until something permanent could be done. When an animal was slain to provide the skins for Adam and Eve, a sacrificial system was begun. It was a system that would allow God and His people to have fellowship once again.

If God was willing to move that quickly to restore fellowship with Adam and Eve, does it make sense that He would move any less quickly to restore fellowship with us? And if the heavenly Father was willing to move that quickly to restore fellowship with sinners, how much more quickly should we move to restore fellowship with those who have wronged us?

The big picture is simply this: People turned their backs on God and God immediately went to work to regain fellowship. These observations from the Old Testament should be enough to convince us that God is a God of love and forgiveness. He forgives because He desires to forgive, not because He is under some constraint. His forgiveness is not handed out on an individual basis depending upon the sin committed. On the contrary, in the Old Testament God set up a system by which *any man or woman could come to Him regardless of the sin committed.* In the New Testament we find that these same principles of forgiveness apply. (In the next chapter we will look at God's permanent solution to the problem of sin.)

HIS WAY OR YOUR WAY?

A major hindrance to the ability to experience God's forgiveness is the unwillingness to accept God's frame of reference concerning sin and the individual's inability to do anything about it. Instead, some people create for themselves a procedure for finding forgiveness and impose it upon God. In time their emotions become so attuned to their own way of thinking that it is almost impossible for them to accept any other way. Usually, their alternate systems underestimate the consequences of sin and overestimate their ability to remedy the situation.

You may be one of these people. I urge you to think about two things. First, God and God alone fully understands the reality of your sinful condition. Only God understands your need in terms of your relationship with Him. Therefore, regardless of what your mind and emotions may tell you, regardless of what may seem fair or unfair, God's plan for forgiveness is the only plan in which you can put your trust with any assurance.

Second, since that is true, are you willing to examine your heart and ask God to reveal any alternative systems you may have been clinging to? Are you willing to lay aside those things and ask God to show you *His* way to true forgiveness?

Cain decided to approach God his way, according to what made sense to him. The result of his decision was disastrous. If you insist on seeking forgiveness any way but God's, the result will be no less disastrous for you. But if you look at your sin and God's provision for dealing with it from His perspective, you will experience freedom that comes with knowing *you are truly forgiven!*

QUESTIONS FOR PERSONAL GROWTH

1. How does sin create a deficit in God's economy? What is required to balance the economy?

2. What does the word *atonement* mean?

3. What does God want more than retribution? Why?

4. What is the major hindrance to experiencing God's forgiveness?

5. Have you been clinging to alternative systems for forgiveness?

Three

THE ONLY SOLUTION

One of my more memorable seminary professors had a practical way of illustrating the concept of grace for his students. At the end of his evangelism course he would hand out the exam with the caution to read it all the way through before beginning to answer it. This caution was written on the exam as well.

As we read through the exam, it became unquestionably clear to each of us that we had not studied nearly enough. The further we read, the worse it became. About halfway through, audible groans could be heard throughout the lecture hall. By the time we were turning to the last page, we were all ready to turn the exam in blank. It was impossible to pass.

On the last page, however, there was a note that read, "You have a choice. You can either complete the exam as given or sign your name at the bottom and in so doing receive an A for this assignment."

Wow! We sat there, stunned. "Was he serious? Just sign it and get an A?" Slowly the point dawned on us, and one by one we turned in our tests and silently filed out of the room. It took the rest of the afternoon for me to get over it. I had the urge to go back and check with him one more time to make sure he was serious.

When I talked with him about it afterward, he shared some of the reactions he had received through the years as he had given the same exam. There were always students who did not follow instructions and began to take the exam without reading it all the way through. Some of them would sweat it out for the entire two hours of class time before reaching the last page. Their ignorance caused them unnecessary anxiety.

Then there were the ones who would read the first two pages, become angry, turn in their paper blank, and storm out of the room. They never realized what was available. As a result, they lost out totally.

One fellow, however, topped them all. He read the entire test, including the note at the end, but he decided to take the exam anyway. He did not want any gifts; he wanted to earn his grade. And he did. He made a C+, which was amazing considering the difficulty of the test. But he could have easily had an A.

ACTIONS AND REACTIONS

This story vividly illustrates many people's reaction to God's solution to sin. Many are like the first group. They spend their lives trying to earn what they discover years later was freely offered to them the whole time. They spend years sweating it out, always wondering if God is listening to their pleas for forgiveness, always wondering if they have finally pushed Him too far. They hope God has forgiven them; they suppose He has. They do all they know to do to be forgiven. But insofar as God is concerned, they do not want to be presumptuous. So they live their lives with doubts.

Many people respond like the second group. They look at God's standard—moral and ethical perfection—and throw their hands up in surrender. *Why even try?* They tell themselves, *I could never live up to all that stuff.* They live the way they please, not expecting anything from God when they die. Often they decide there is no God. Their acknowledged inability to live up to His standard drives them to this conclusion. Instead of living under constant pressure and guilt, they choose to completely abandon the standard. What a shock it will be for them when they stand before God and understand for the first time what was available had they only asked!

Then there is the guy who took the test anyway. I meet people like him all the time who are unwilling to simply receive God's gift of forgiveness. Striking out to do it on their own, they strive to earn enough points with God to give them the right to look to their own goodness as a means of pardon and forgiveness. They constantly work at "evening the score" with God through their good works. "Sure, I have my faults," they say. "But God does not expect anyone to be perfect."

When it comes to forgiveness, there is no room for boasting in one's own ability. As we will see, forgiveness is not a team effort. It is not a matter of God's doing His part and us doing ours. Unlike my professor's test, in God's economy anything less than 100 percent is failing.

THE BOTTOM LINE

The bottom line is that through Christ, God did away with the problem of sin insofar as its ability to keep us from having a relationship with Him. Let's examine how He did that.

As we have discussed, the entrance of sin into the world

meant that members of the human race lost physical life (a gradual process) and righteous standing before God. Fellowship with
the sinless Creator was interrupted.

There was another angle to sin and its relationship to
death. God demanded the life of the sinner: "For the wages
of sin is death" (Rom. 6:23). Sin earned the sinner death.

Although sin deserved immediate action on God's part,
God in His mercy did not immediately judge humankind.
He chose to suspend judgment to give His people a second
chance.

Time is the key factor. Every individual has the length of
a lifetime to restore a personal relationship with God. Once
life ends, however, judgment comes: "And inasmuch as it is
appointed for men to die once and after this comes judgment" (Heb. 9:27).

Because of His unexplainable love, God desired (and still
desires) to have fellowship with men and women. As we saw in
Chapter 2, He established a temporary system through which
fellowship could be restored and maintained and sin could be
covered—but not forgiven. Sin would have to be forgiven
before the problem of sin could be solved once and for all.
That is where Christ entered the picture.

GOD'S ECONOMY

To understand how the coming of Christ facilitated the forgiveness of sin, we must understand some basics about the
nature of God. God's righteousness, that is, His sinlessness
and holiness, by definition set up a standard that all those
who would have fellowship with Him must meet. To put it
another way, certain things must be true about people to be
acceptable to God.

When I say this standard is set up by definition of His righteous nature, I mean that God did not arbitrarily establish this standard as we would establish the rules of a game. If that were the case, He could just change His standard and everybody would be acceptable. God's righteous standard flows from His unalterable nature.

God's righteousness can be compared to fire. Certain things must be true of any material that is to survive being exposed to fire. The nature of the fire determines what will and will not last.

God's righteousness can be compared to water. Certain things must be true of any animal that is to live underwater. The nature of water demands that these things be true. Any animal that does not meet these standards will not survive. Furthermore, the standards cannot be changed because they flow from the very nature of water.

So it is with God. His nature demands that certain things be true of those who desire to have uninterrupted fellowship with Him and who desire to someday dwell in His very presence. Specifically, His nature demands sinlessness, or perfection, but the presence of sin makes us unacceptable to Him. Paul expresses this concept when he writes: "For all have sinned and fall short of the glory of God" (Rom. 3:23).

Our sin causes us to "fall short." Our sin disqualifies us in light of God's standard. Sin puts us in a relationship with God wherein we owe Him something. We must pay for what we have done much like common criminals must repay society for the crimes committed. Thus, the solution must in some way remove the consequences of our sin and restore us to a state in which our sin is no longer counted against us. Somehow, what was done through sin must be undone. So, how can that happen? How can the sinful be made the sinless?

ALL RIGHT ALREADY!

By now you are probably wondering why we don't move along a little faster. I have repeated some significant points because we need to understand as much as is humanly possible about God's forgiveness. Until it all clearly fits together, we are not likely to abandon the unbiblical ways of thinking we have grown comfortable with through the years. Until we see how the whole thing fits together, it will be difficult for us to change our prayer habits. And until we are confronted with (and have accepted) God's unconditional goodness to us, we will have a difficult time forgiving others.

NOW YOU SEE IT . . .
NOW YOU DON'T

To help us better understand how God can undo what has been done insofar as our sinfulness is concerned, we can look at one aspect of our present legal system. If people are convicted of a serious crime, such as a felony, they lose their civil rights. They are not allowed to vote. They are not allowed to hold public office. These rights can be restored only through the granting of a pardon by a governor of a state or by the president if it is a federal case.

The interesting thing about a pardon is that it is not conditional upon guilt. That is, when someone receives a pardon, it is not necessarily an indication of innocence. It simply means that the person does not have to pay the penalty for the offense; there are no legal or civil consequences. For example, when President Ford pardoned Richard Nixon, it was out of respect for the office he had held, not because Nixon was proved to be innocent. According to the law, then, a governor or the president in effect has the power to allow a guilty individual to go free; the crime is never paid for; the person suffers none of the regular consequences.

Like persons convicted of a felony, we lost our citizenship. Sin resulted in the forfeiture of our right to enter the kingdom of God. Like a governor, God has the power to pardon those who are guilty. There is one major difference, though. In our system of law a crime does not have to be paid for. A governor can pardon a convicted person, and that is the end of it. But the nature of God requires that those who dwell in His presence must be sinless, which means we must have committed no sins or have no sin that has not been paid for. God's nature will not allow Him to simply overlook sin. Sin carries with it a penalty that must be paid. The author of Hebrews sums it up this way: "Without the shedding of blood there is no forgiveness" (Heb. 9:22 NIV).

Think of it like this. A builder cannot make the payments on his bank loan. He goes to the president of the bank and apologizes for being so irresponsible. He asks the president to forgive him and then expresses an interest in doing business with the bank in the future. Regardless of how kind and understanding the president of the bank is, the nature of his job restricts him from simply patting the builder on the back and saying, "No hard feelings. We understand. Forget about the money and try to be more careful next time." It does not work that way. The builder will not be in good standing with the bank until his debt is paid.

Our sin and the debt that resulted left us in a position wherein we needed both *pardon* and *payment*. The situation was hopeless. We did not have the potential to regain for ourselves what was necessary to make us acceptable to God. It was checkmate, the game was over; there were no more moves for us to make. And it was nobody's fault but our own. Yet in our darkest hour, God gave us an extra Player and, in doing so, a second chance.

BAD NEWS/GOOD NEWS

As you think about what has been said so far, you will notice that neither the *degree* of sin nor the *quantity* of sin has been mentioned. That is because both are irrelevant. Yet if you are like many people I talk to every week, these are the two issues you may be wrestling with as you question God's willingness or ability to forgive you. The bad news is the good news. It took only one less-than-perfect move to forfeit the right to a relationship with God. That is the bad news. The good news is that there are no degrees of separation.

Perhaps this example will clarify what I mean. It is similar to the situation of two people who lost their jobs. One was fired for coming into work late; the other for stealing from the cash register and falsifying his time card. What the first guy did was not even in the same league with the actions of the second. But fired is fired, and neither had a job.

If you can understand that everyone is in the same boat in terms of separation from God, it will be far easier for you to accept God's solution to the sin problem. Paul expresses the same idea:

So then as through one transgression there resulted condemnation to *all* men, even so through one act of righteousness there resulted justification of life to *all* men. For as through the one man's disobedience the *many* were made sinners, even so through the obedience of the One the *many* will be made righteous. (Rom. 5:18–19, emphasis mine)

Paul lumps everybody into one of two categories, *condemned* or *justified*. He does not mention quantity or quality of sins.

Another truth in this passage is extremely important to recognize. We have seen how our sin incurred for us a debt that was nonnegotiable in view of the nature of God and was unpayable in regard to our ability to pay it. Yet what Paul implies in these verses, and is straightforward about saying in other places, is that just as one man's (Adam's) sin had the potential to affect every man and woman, so one Man's (Christ's) righteous act had the potential to undo what had been done by Adam. If one man had the potential to damage the entire human race, certainly the Son of God had the potential to make everything right. In other words, Christ had the ability to cancel our indebtedness by assuming our debt and paying the penalty that was required.

PAID IN FULL

Using the analogy of indebtedness when talking about sin and its consequences fits perfectly with the New Testament's approach to the subject. Paul writes,

> And when you were dead in your transgressions and the uncircumcision of your flesh, He made you alive together with Him, having forgiven us all our transgressions . . .

And then he illustrates what he has just written by adding:

> . . . having canceled out the certificate of debt consisting of decrees against us and which was hostile to us; and He has taken it out of the way, having nailed it to the cross. (Col. 2:13–14)

Paul's use of the word *having* implies the idea of means. We could restate verse 13 this way: "He made you alive together with Him by means of forgiving us all our transgressions." Forgiveness is the way in which God makes us alive.

The phrase "having forgiven us all our transgressions" means the same thing as "having canceled out the certificate of debt consisting of decrees against us." Forgiveness, then, is the cancellation of a debt.

Paul is referring to a practice familiar to his first-century audience. In those days a man who owed another man would write out a *certificate of debt*. The certificate would include all that was owed along with the terms of payment. The debtor, the lender, and a witness would sign the document.

In a sense each of us had a certificate of debt against us, and Christ's death canceled the certificate. Paul says, "He has taken it out of the way, having nailed it to the cross." Often an ex-debtor would nail up his canceled certificate of debt in a public place so all would know his debt had been paid. Paul picks up on this practice and says that our debt was nailed to the cross with Christ, signifying that it had been paid in full: It was no longer legally binding.

If we have correctly understood Paul's analogy, there should be no question that total forgiveness of sin comes through Christ. And that includes all sins—the ones we have already committed and the ones we will commit. From the perspective of the Cross, they were all future. And it was from that perspective they were dealt with. So Paul could say to believers he had never met, "He made you alive together with Him, having forgiven us all our transgressions" (Col. 2:13). He did not need to know how many sins the Colossian believers had committed. He did not need to know the nature of their sins. All he needed to know was that they had approached God for forgiveness through Christ. That was enough then—and that is enough for us today!

I can say to you, with perfect assurance, that if you have trusted Christ's death on the cross to be the payment for your sins, your sins are forgiven. I don't know you any more than Paul knew all the Colossians or Ephesians or Romans who read his letters. But it does not matter. We are all condemned apart from Christ, and we can all be forgiven through Him. No matter what you have done, how many times you have done it, or who you hurt in the process, God has forgiven you.

If doubts about your particular situation remain in your mind, it should be obvious that you are still thinking about forgiveness according to your own artificial standards. If what I have said thus far is true, through Christ you have forgiveness (Eph. 1:7). Right now as you read, you are a forgiven child of God. The guilt you continue to carry around because of past sins is unnecessary. Later I'll explain how to deal with false guilt. But to begin with, you must accept the truth about your past hopelessness as well as your present forgiven state: *You are forgiven.*

"MY GOD, MY GOD"

At this point you may be asking, "If our sin demanded a death—but this death involved eternal separation from God—how could Christ pay the penalty for our sin and still sit at the Father's right hand? If He took our place, it would seem He should go to hell. That is where we were heading, wasn't it?" In searching for answers, we are once again confronted with God's insatiable desire to restore fellowship with humankind. As we will see, Christ did have to suffer the punishment we would have had to suffer.

Mark described the events surrounding the crucifixion of Jesus:

> And when the sixth hour had come, darkness fell over the whole land until the ninth hour. And at the ninth hour Jesus cried out with a loud voice, "Eloi, Eloi, lama sabachthani?" which is translated, "My God, My God, why hast Thou forsaken Me?" (Mark 15:33–34)

While hanging on the cross, Christ experienced for our sake separation from His heavenly Father. The separation was so deep that Christ even addressed Him differently. Until that time He had spoken of God as His Father. All of a sudden He cried out, "My God." There was no longer the intimacy, the warmth, or the closeness. Gone was the assurance He had just a few hours earlier when He said to His disciples,

> Behold, an hour is coming, and has already come, for you to be scattered, each to his own home, and to leave Me alone; and yet I am not alone, because the Father is with Me. (John 16:32)

Why the change? Because sin required separation from the Sinless One. In taking on the responsibility of our sin (2 Cor. 5:21), Christ voluntarily put Himself in a position in which He no longer had fellowship with the heavenly Father. Just as Adam was cast out of the Garden, so Christ, in a sense, was cast out of His privileged position with God.

Think for a moment. What if the person you loved the most—the person whose approval you valued more than anyone's—suddenly walked out on you? You may have experienced pain just like that, the type of pain you would not wish on your worst enemy. Yet Christ volunteered to suffer that kind of pain multiplied ten thousand times because it was the only way God could get you back. It was the only way He could arrange for your forgiveness. God wanted you, and He wanted you badly!

After becoming sin for our sakes and suffering the punishment we deserved, Christ was accepted back into fellowship with His heavenly Father:

> But He, having offered one sacrifice for sins for all time, sat down at the right hand of God, waiting from that time onward until His enemies be made a footstool for His feet. For by one offering He has perfected for all time those who are sanctified. (Heb. 10:12–14)

Christ was accepted back into fellowship based upon His own righteousness. He needed no sacrifice for His sin. He had no debt that needed paying, because He was sinless. He had the right through His own merit to sit at the right hand of God.

TAKE IT OR LEAVE IT

There we have it. Christ is God's solution for dealing with sin. Only through Christ can we find forgiveness. But once it has been found, it is a settled issue—past sin, present sin, and future sin. The details of what we have done, why we did it, and how many times we did it are irrelevant. Sin is sin; lost is lost; paid is paid; forgiven is forgiven. Either we have it, or we don't.

Are there sins from your past that continue to hang over you like a dark cloud? When you pray, does something inside you cause you to doubt that God is going to listen to you because of your past? Do you feel that your potential for the

kingdom of God has been destroyed because of your past disobedience? If you answered yes to any of these questions, you
have not yet come to grips with God's solution to your sin.
You are still holding on to a way of thinking that will keep you
in bondage the rest of your life. You have set yourself up to
live a defeated life in which you will never know your potential for the kingdom of God.

I want you to be free. More important, God wants you to
be free. And because He does, He sacrificed what was dearest
to Him. I encourage you to meditate on the concepts of this
chapter. Ask God to sink them deep into your subconscious
so that they become the grid through which you interpret the
experiences of life. Not until you are able to see yourself as a
forgiven child of God will you begin to enjoy the fellowship
that the death of His Son made possible.

QUESTIONS FOR PERSONAL GROWTH

1. Name three ways people may react to God's offer of forgiveness. What is wrong with these reactions?

2. Explain how God's forgiveness is like an executive pardon. Why is the guilt of the person who is pardoned *not* an issue?

3. Why does the *degree* or *quantity* of sin make no difference in the judgment of guilt? Why is forgiveness a settled issue—even for future sins—once it has been found?

4. What past sins are still hanging over your head? Have you come to grips with God's solution?

Four

FAITH AND FORGIVENESS

One of the most difficult habits for me to break was playing what I call the time game. It went like this. I would sin. I would feel guilty. I would ask God to forgive me. Then, depending on the magnitude of the sin, I would allow a certain amount of time to pass before I would ask God for things again. Sometimes I would wait an hour. Sometimes I would wait until the next day. I realize now that this was my way of punishing myself. But on the conscious level, I did it out of respect for God. I mean, God is forgiving and all that, but I felt I needed to give Him a little time to cool off before I started right back in with Him; I could not go on as if nothing happened. I understood all about the theology of forgiveness, but what I knew in my head had not taken hold of my heart and my emotions and my actions.

Many people share this problem. They nod their heads in agreement as the preacher expounds on the unconditional love of God and His desire to restore fellowship with lost men and women. Then you ask them, "Do you think God has really forgiven you?" And they reply, "I hope so," or "I guess we really don't know until the end." For many Christians, a seed of doubt remains that all their personal sins are really forgiven, that God is genuinely not holding anything against them.

Until we are sure, until we settle the issue of forgiveness once and for all, two things will always be true. First, we will never have much confidence when we petition our heavenly Father. We will always feel that God is holding something against us. Second, we will put others on the same scale we put ourselves on. Since we are always trying to do something to ensure our forgiveness, we will subconsciously pressure others to perform to gain our forgiveness. We will have a tendency to remind others of their failures and their need to make up for them in some way.

A believer who functions in a "payback" mode in relation to personal standing before God is like a man who wins a car and continues to walk everywhere he goes. People comment on how beautiful it is, and he agrees. He keeps it clean, he reads the owner's manual several times until he is thoroughly familiar with every facet of the car. Yet it does not accomplish for him what it was intended to accomplish. And it is all his fault. The car is no less his. But practically speaking, he might as well not own it. So it is with the believer who does not accept the forgiveness of God.

MAKING SURE

God wants us to live with perfect assurance that we are completely forgiven. To facilitate this, He has provided directions for making sure His gift of forgiveness has been applied to each individual's situation. In Chapter 3 we looked at the mechanics of forgiveness, how it all fits together. In this chapter we will look closely at the door through which each individual must pass to become a partaker of God's forgiveness.

My purpose here is twofold: to provide assurance for some and instruction for others. I want those of you who have passed through this door to walk away with perfect assurance that you have no need to ever doubt your forgiveness again, because you have done it God's way. For those of you who may never have understood exactly how to get in on God's plan for forgiveness, I want to clarify it so that you too can share in it.

If the last chapter can be thought of as putting together the elements of a contract, this chapter can be approached like the signing, the time when the lawyer points to the line at the bottom and hands you the pen to sign your name. Only then do the conditions of the legal document apply to you.

In the same way, God has left us instructions as to how we are to sign His contract for forgiveness. Yet many Christians have a tendency to complicate them, add to them, and attempt to redefine the terms. But if what we have seen so far is true, that God intensely desires fellowship with us, it makes sense that He would keep the instructions as simple as possible.

THE DOTTED LINE

The Old Testament Levitical laws delineated how an individual became a beneficiary of God's offer for atonement. Let's look once again at the sacrificial system:

> And he shall lay his hand on the head of the burnt offering, that it may be accepted for him to make atonement on his behalf. (Lev. 1:4)

A man had to bring a sacrifice that met certain standards and sacrifice it on the altar. As I pointed out in Chapter 2, not only did the one making the sacrifice have to bring an animal, but he also had to place his hand on its head as it was sacrificed. Thus, he identified with the dying animal, and God's promise of atonement was appropriated to his account.

What, then, is the New Testament equivalent to the placing of the hand on the head of the sacrifice? Just as the Old Testament saints had to have a way of appropriating God's promises concerning forgiveness, so must we.

The point of identification for New Testament Christians is *faith*. Perhaps a better word is *trust*. To make God's gift of forgiveness our own, we must exercise faith. We must trust Him to apply His work through Christ to our account when we sign on the dotted line of the certificate of pardon.

Now we need to consider something. Do we realize that every time we play the time game, or whatever games we play with God, we are turning our backs on His means of ensuring our forgiveness and creating our own? What is worse, we are abandoning a system of faith for a system of works.

When we punish ourselves, whether it is by depriving ourselves of something or doing more than what is expected in some area, we treat God as if He requires some penance for our sin. We act as if a demonstration of our sorrow earns forgiveness for us. We may feel better about ourselves when we demonstrate our sorrow in some way, but self-punishment has nothing to do with God's willingness to forgive. It has nothing to do with forgiveness at all. Yet every time we consciously or subconsciously work out some trade-off with God in regard to sin, we are abandoning His way for our way.

If we have placed our trust in God's system of forgiveness,

we live in a forgiven state. From God's perspective, that means there is no difference between the sins we have committed, are committing, and will commit. None! Remember, forgiven is forgiven. In one sense, living in a state of forgiveness can be compared to having a checking account with unlimited funds available. In that financial condition we do not have to ask someone else to pay our debts for us. It would be impossible for us to incur debts as long as we write checks and continue to draw on our account.

This is exactly Paul's point when he writes:

> And the Law came in that the transgression might increase, but where sin increased, grace abounded all the more, that, as sin reigned in death, even so grace might reign through righteousness to eternal life through Jesus Christ our Lord. (Rom. 5:20–21)

There is always more grace than there is sin. Regardless of what is done or how many times it is done, it is already covered by God's grace. That is His willingness to consider it paid for in view of Christ's death. To work out our own system of merit is to say that God's grace is not sufficient for our sin, that He needs our help in dealing with our sin.

Our natural tendency is toward a work ethic in terms of our forgiveness. We find it difficult not to do *something* on our behalf. We are quick to give lip service to concepts such as *forgiveness comes through faith* and *we can do nothing to merit forgiveness*, but when it comes down to everyday living, we revert to a works-plus-faith system. That being the case, we need to understand the nature of faith and how it functions as the door into the realm of forgiveness. When we have made this idea our own, our behavior will be transformed. Our relationships with God and with others will be in accordance with what God intends for us, not what we intend for ourselves.

"I Believe! I Think?"

What is faith? What does it involve? These may seem to be somewhat elementary questions, but Christians answer in various ways and rarely do they respond with answers that fit the biblical data. A whole host of people seem to be confused about whether or not they have *really* believed. On the other hand, some people are certain that they believe, but when pressed for details, they are not exactly sure *what* they believe; the content of their faith is undefined. Confusion or a lack of assurance in this area logically leads to confusion and doubts about forgiveness as well.

The use of the term *believe* in connection with forgiveness is not parallel to common uses of the term. For instance, someone might say, "I believe it will snow tonight." In that case the term *believe* carries with it the idea of "calculated hope." That is, there is no guarantee it will snow; it is just a personal impression. Or a person might say, "I believe in God." In this case *believe* denotes mental assent to an idea. There is no sense of trust or commitment, just an acceptance of facts. (For a more complete discussion of this idea, see H. Phillip Hook, "A Biblical Definition of Saving Faith." *Bibliotheca Sacra* [April 1964].)

If we take these two unbiblical uses of the term *believe* and apply them to a discussion of forgiveness, we can understand how an individual can express belief in something and yet have no personal assurance. A person can say, "I believe God forgave me of my sin," and then turn right around and say, "I hope I am forgiven." There really is no contradiction for the person who uses the term to refer to a calculated hope.

In the same way, an individual who understands faith as mental assent to facts can say, "I believe God offers forgiveness through Christ," and yet have never had God's forgiveness applied to personal sin. Think about that. A man or a woman can verbally express faith and not be forgiven. The problem is that neither has expressed biblical faith.

BIBLICAL FAITH

In discussing the meaning of biblical faith, the term *trust* should be substituted whenever *faith* or *believe* is being used in connection with forgiveness or salvation in general. *Webster's Third New International Dictionary* defines *trust* as: "assured reliance on some person or thing; a confident dependence on the character, ability, strength, or truth of someone or something."

The concept of trust denotes personal involvement. It assumes a relationship of some sort between the one expressing trust and the person or thing being trusted. The difference between belief and trust is the difference between acknowledging that the bridge is capable of holding a person's weight, and actually walking out on the bridge. The former is simply the acknowledgment of something, with no involvement on the part of the one expressing faith; the latter is actual dependence.

Biblical faith, the type of faith that serves as the door to forgiveness, assumes a relationship of actual dependence and reliance. To state it in *Webster's* terms, biblical faith, or trust, is "the assured reliance on God: a confident dependence on the character, ability, strength, and truth of God and His promises."

The biblical support for this understanding of the term *believe* comes from a grammatical construct that occurs repeatedly when faith is spoken of in connection with forgiveness and salvation. This construct consists of the Greek word that means "believe" followed by a little word that is translated "in" or "on," depending on the context of the passage and the Bible version used.

I emphasize the use of these two words together because the expression was original with the New Testament writers. They used it forty-five times. Yet there is no parallel to this construction in either the Greek version of the Old Testament or the secular Greek literature of the day. (For more on this, see Gerald F. Hawthorne, "The Concept of Faith in the Fourth Gospel." *Bibliotheca Sacra* [April 1959].)

This means that the New Testament writers had to develop terminology as original as their message. So John wrote the following:

> But as many as received Him, to them He gave the right to become children of God, even to those who *believe in* His name. (John 1:12, emphasis mine)

> Now when He was in Jerusalem at the Passover, during the feast, many *believed in* His name, beholding His signs which He was doing. (John 2:23, emphasis mine)

The object of biblical faith, as regards forgiveness, is always the person or words of Jesus. By "object" I mean what people are being asked to put their faith in. For example, in the statement "Trust the car to get you there," the car is the object of faith. This is an important point because many people have faith, but it is directed in all sorts of inappropriate directions— or no direction at all.

The object of forgiving faith must be Christ, not simply God, the goodness of God, or faith itself. Jesus points to this truth when He says,

Let not your heart be troubled; believe in God, believe also in Me . . . I am the way, and the truth, and the life; no one comes to the Father, but through Me. (John 14:1, 6)

Jesus parallels *believing in Him* with *believing in God.* Then He turns right around and says that "no one" gets to God except through Him.

I mention this because many people have faith *in God,* yet have never expressed faith *in Christ.* I meet men especially who express faith in God, but they leave Christ out of the picture altogether. They have faith, but the object of their faith is wrong or, perhaps I should say, limited.

Many people have faith in another god. They often respond by saying something to the effect that, "All religions lead to God; you choose your way, and I'll choose mine." This sounds so just and fair. And once again there is a genuine expression of faith. But it is faith man's way, not God's. It is real faith without a real foundation. It is sincere, but uninformed, faith. Forgiveness is available only to the man or woman who has put personal trust in Christ. For faith to accomplish its intended purpose, it must be focused in the right direction.

The New Testament writers were calling people to place their trust in the person of Jesus Christ for the forgiveness of their sins and the promise of eternal life. They were asking people to rely on or depend on Christ as the way to God and thus to forgiveness of sin. It was more than acknowledging that Christ was from God. It was more than hoping that what He said was true. It was a personal commitment to dependency upon Him for forgiveness. It was a matter of casting hopes for eternity upon the claims and promises of Jesus Christ. Such faith was (and still is) the way to forgiveness.

For God so loved the world, that He gave His only begotten Son, that whoever *believes in* Him should not perish, but have eternal life. (John 3:16, emphasis mine)

APPROPRIATING THE GIFT

God's gift of forgiveness must be appropriated; that is, it must be accepted on an individual basis. Although it is a universal offer, it has no effect on the sin debt of a man or a woman who has not personally put trust in Christ. It is like a paycheck that is never picked up; it is like a gift certificate that is not redeemed; it is like a lifeline that is ignored by a drowning person.

Christ creatively communicated the concept of appropriation. Through the use of word pictures and parables, He drove home His point to "put your trust in Me." He told the woman at the well to ask for "living water" (John 4:10). He instructed the Jews to come to Him to receive "life" (John 5:40). He told one group they would have to "eat the flesh of the Son of Man and drink His blood" (John 6:53). To the leaders of the Jews, He said, "If anyone keeps My word he shall never see death" (John 8:51). He used every conceivable illustration to show His audience that they needed to personally and individually appropriate God's gift of eternal life for themselves.

Christ constantly reiterated the need to appropriate His offer because the Jewish mind-set was such that the Jews believed they were automatically included in God's plan simply because of their nationality. Their confusion was similar to the confusion I find in many people today. Most people want to avoid the subject of accountability to God. Hearing the gospel may be bearable, but making a decision to place their trust in Christ to be the payment for their sin is going a step too far. They would much rather go on thinking about God as some benevolent force in the sky who loves everybody and who would not dare send anybody to hell. What they overlook is their responsibility to appropriate, through faith, God's gift of forgiveness.

WHAT ABOUT YOU?

That brings us to some important questions. Has there been a time in your life when you personally placed your trust in the death of Christ to be the payment for your sin? Have you appropriated His payment for your debt? Have you tasted the living water? Have you walked through the door that leads to salvation? Have you received eternal life?

Remember, *knowing* the truth is not enough. Understanding what Christ did is only the first step. Forgiveness comes through *trusting* in Christ. Regardless of what you have done or how many times you have done it or who you hurt in the process, complete forgiveness is available if you are willing to receive it. But it is available only through the death of Christ.

If, on the other hand, you know that you have placed your trust in the death of Christ for the payment of your sin, I can say to you with full assurance, "You are forgiven!"—past, present, and future. No more saying, "I hope so" or "I think so." You can say, "I know so!"

MEMORIALS AND REMINDERS

You may be thinking: *That is easy for you to say, but I am plagued by memories of the past. Every time I pray I think about the things I have done, and I feel alienated from God. I cannot pray with any confidence or assurance.*

If that is your situation, let me offer a practical exercise that will turn things around for you. First, you must settle in your mind once and for all that your sins are forgiven; that God is in no way holding them against you; that from His perspective, they are no longer obstacles to fellowship. That takes care of the mind aspect, now for the emotions.

Second, you must begin to view your past failures as reminders of God's grace. Your past sins should become memorials to the grace of God in your life. When Satan accuses you of being unworthy because of things you have done in the past, you can respond by saying (and I recommend actually speaking out loud), "That is exactly right. I did do that, and that's not all. But before I ever committed my first sin Jesus Christ died and paid for my sins—not just the ones you have reminded me of—all of them. Now they stand in my past as memorials, reminders, of God's goodness and grace toward me. Thanks for the reminder."

This may seem like just a mental exercise, but more important, it is also a confession of truth. It confesses the truth you need to combat the lies of Satan. In time you will be able to rejoice at the thought of your past in connection with the grace of God as it was demonstrated at Calvary. Soon what once destroyed your assurance will become your greatest source of assurance.

As we close this chapter, I want to ask you one more time if you know for sure that you have expressed personal trust in the death of Christ for the payment of your sins. If not, there is a sense in which God just slid His eternal contract in front of you and now waits for you to sign. You can do that right where you are by simply confessing your sins and telling Him that you are putting your trust in His Son's death to be the payment for your sins. Once you do that, *you are forgiven*!

QUESTIONS FOR PERSONAL GROWTH

1. Explain the time game and give some examples of how you may have played it.

2. How does *faith* function as the door to forgiveness?

3. Biblical faith involves faith in the person or words of whom? Explain why "faith in God" is a limited faith.

4. How is forgiveness appropriated? Have you personally trusted in the death of Christ for payment of your sins?

Five

OUR FORGIVING FATHER

When my children were younger, we would have family meetings to discuss chores, summer plans, or other family business. Although they were for the most part planning sessions, when I would "call" the meetings, my kids would usually look at me with great concern and say, "Did we do something wrong?"

I was puzzled by their reaction until my wife pointed out that the tone of my voice was very serious when I announced the meeting, much like it was when I disciplined the kids. So it was natural for them to respond the way they did.

My kids' attitude is similar to that of many believers when they have to "do business" with God. They come to Him confident of only one thing—they have blown it, they have done something wrong, and forgotten to ask God to forgive them. They know all about the substitutionary death of Christ and all that, but they picture God as an angry old man who just puts up with them. I have talked with folks who even make a differentiation between Christ's attitude toward them and the Father's. They view Christ as the Friend who is working to hold back the wrath of God the Father. They understand Christ's role, as the One who paid for their sins, to mean that He is the only One preventing God from giving them what they really deserve. The assumption is that God wishes He could give them what they deserve, in spite of Christ.

You may never have pictured God the Father exactly like that. But how do you picture Him when you think about your sin? What do you think His expression is when you come to Him with the same old sin time and time again? What do you think His attitude is toward you in light of your failures? What do your emotions tell you when you contemplate these questions? Like most Christians, you would probably acknowledge that God loves you. But do you think He *likes* you? Or do you think He just puts up with you because, after all, His Son did die for you?

For many people, these are especially difficult questions. The term *Father* does not bring with it feelings of love and acceptance. Instead it conjures up feelings of fear, dread, hurt, and disappointment. I have counseled with enough people to know that these feelings associated with an earthly father have the potential of robbing them of the assurance of forgiveness the heavenly Father sacrificed so deeply for them to experience.

We have seen a great deal of biblical evidence illustrating that our heavenly Father desires to have fellowship with each of us. He desired that while we were still sinners, still separated by the debt of sin. Paul writes, "But God demonstrates His own love toward us, in that while we were yet sinners, Christ died for us" (Rom. 5:8). Until all aspects of this verse sink deep into our emotional being, we will never be free of the feelings of condemnation that accompany sin. The strategy that secured our forgiveness was God's idea; He initiated it. He wants us for His very own.

So What's New?

We are not the first generation to struggle with a distorted view of God's attitude toward sinners. The Jews of Jesus' day had the same misperception. From the premise that God could not tolerate sin along with the guidelines of the Ten Commandments, they developed a system to rate where people stood with God based on the degree of their sin. The worse the sin, the less acceptable a person was. In time this thinking developed to the point where God was perceived as "despising" sinners altogether.

In addition, those whose job or position in life kept them from remaining ceremonially clean as prescribed in Leviticus were considered unacceptable. Shepherds, tax collectors, and butchers were included in this category.

As a result, two mind-sets polarized the Jews of Jesus' day. One group—the majority of the people—felt as if God would never accept them because they could not live righteous and ceremonially clean lives. The other group thought their personal righteousness was enough to make them acceptable. They looked down upon and despised the others, the "sinners."

To correct this thinking, Jesus told a series of parables. The last in the series we know as the parable of the prodigal son. Christ's motivation in telling this parable was to explain to His contemporaries His Father's true attitude toward sinners. We know this from the way the parable is introduced:

Now all the tax-gatherers and the sinners were coming near Him to listen to Him. And both the Pharisees and the scribes began to grumble, saying, "This man receives sinners and eats with them." And He told them this parable. (Luke 15:1–3)

The religious leaders could not understand how a Man who said He was from God could be so attractive to and attracted to such unholy, unclean people. They thought, *God has rejected these people. So why does this prophet spend so much time with them?* Christ's actions did not fit with their notion of God the Father's attitude toward sinners. So Christ set out to straighten them out.

CHANGING THE PICTURE

By looking at this insightful parable, we can pick up on God's attitude toward sinners and His motivation for sending Christ to die. I believe it is the best illustration of the forgiving nature of our heavenly Father in the whole Bible.

It is my prayer that through this chapter God will begin to deal with you on an emotional level so that whatever is keeping you from experiencing the joy and peace of knowing you are forgiven will be put to rest. Whether you are a victim of incorrect teaching or you were mistreated by your earthly father—whatever the stumbling block may be—God wants to take it out of the way and flood you with the assurance of His forgiveness and acceptance. He wants you to live with a sense of security and intimacy with Him.

Take some time to refamiliarize yourself with the parable.

A certain man had two sons; and the younger of them said to his father, "Father, give me the share of the estate that falls to me." And he divided his wealth between them.

And not many days later, the younger son gathered everything together and went on a journey into a distant country, and there he squandered his estate with loose living.

Now when he had spent everything, a severe famine occurred in that country, and he began to be in need. And he went and attached himself to one of the citizens of that country, and he sent him into his fields to feed swine. And he was longing to fill his stomach with the pods that the swine were eating, and no one was giving anything to him.

But when he came to his senses, he said, "How many of my father's hired men have more than enough bread, but I am dying here with hunger! I will get up and go to my father, and will say to him, "Father, I have sinned against heaven, and in your sight; I am no longer worthy to be called your son; make me as one of your hired men.'"

And he got up and came to his father. But while he was still a long way off, his father saw him, and felt compassion for him, and ran and embraced him, and kissed him. And the son said to him, "Father, I have sinned against heaven and in your sight; I am no longer worthy to be called your son." But the father said to his slaves, "Quickly bring out the best robe and put it on him, and put a ring on his hand and sandals on his feet; and bring the fattened calf, kill it, and let us eat and be merry." (Luke 15:11–23)

Jesus gives us this parable of the lost son to help us understand God the Father's attitude toward us when we sin against Him. Since He illustrates His point by reference to a father-son relationship where the son has sinned against the father, it should be obvious that the message is for those who are already of the household of faith, that is, believers. It is particularly aimed at those persons living under the awesome load of uncertainty of knowing they have displeased God.

A WORST-CASE SCENARIO

When we understand the culture of the day, we see that Jesus could not have pictured the prodigal in a more degrading manner. First of all, in his selfish egotism he asked for his share of the inheritance. The custom was for the father to give the inheritance at the time he chose. It would have been unheard of for a son, especially a younger son, to ask for his inheritance. Jesus' audience would have viewed his actions as a sign of great disrespect, maybe even as grounds for disinheritance.

Second, he took it all and left. The custom would have been for him to stick around and care for his aging parents. Sons were to make sure that their fathers were buried properly and that their mothers were provided for. This son took off with no regard for his family. Again, his behavior would have been disturbing to Christ's first-century audience.

Third, he spent his entire inheritance in a relatively short time. His father had taken a lifetime to accumulate it, and it represented years of hard work and wise stewardship. Yet the younger son spent it all on short-lived pleasure. It would seem that Jesus could have added nothing to make the son sound any more disreputable. The father had every right in the world to write him off as a sluggard and an embarrassment to the family.

But Jesus took him even one step further. After he had run out of money and the famine hit, he did the most despicable thing a Jewish man could do—he took a job caring for hogs. Not cows or sheep, but pigs. Jesus could have said nothing about the young man that would have been more horrifying to the Pharisees.

WHY SO BAD?

Why did Jesus picture the prodigal in such an extreme fashion? He was trying to help us understand something basic about forgiveness. The young man's sinfulness was such that there was nothing left in him that could motivate his father to forgive him. His father forgave him because it was his nature to love and thus to forgive. And that was Jesus' point exactly.

Like the father in the parable, God forgives because it is His nature to forgive. Nothing we can do on our own can prompt God to forgive us. It is His character that moves Him, not ours. Earlier we discussed God's initiating the forgiving process, and Jesus' vivid word picture of a father and son portrayed just that.

A SURPRISING RESPONSE

When Jesus got to the part of the story where he described the son's desire to return home, I can only imagine the Pharisees' feelings as they thought about what they would do if they had a son who behaved in such a manner. No doubt they were shocked at how Jesus closed the story.

The son finally realized the futility of his ways and decided to go home. There was no mention of his cleaning himself up. As far as we know, he did not even attempt to make himself presentable to his father. He just headed home in the most despicable condition possible.

When the father saw his son coming down the road, he ran toward him, hugged him, and kissed him. He showered his affection upon the dirty, bedraggled, hog-feeding son of his who had squandered his inheritance and embarrassed the family. He seemed unconcerned about where his son had been or what he had done; his focus was on his son who had returned.

HOW FAR IS TOO FAR?

This "surprise ending" reveals several marvelous facets of God's attitude toward returning sinners. First, *our heavenly Father's love has no limits.* If there had been a limit on how far the father was willing to stretch before cutting his son off completely, certainly the young man had gone too far. He did everything wrong.

The point is clear. A man or a woman cannot go so far that God's love and forgiveness are no longer offered. The father would have accepted the son back at any time. The implication, therefore, is that the son was forgiven before he ever returned. From the father's perspective, there was no condemnation. That is why he accepted his son back into the family so quickly.

Regardless of what you have done, you have not stretched God beyond His limits. His love knows no limits. Your sin was dealt with two thousand years ago when Christ died. As far as He is concerned, you live in a state of forgiveness.

HOW LONG IS TOO LONG?

We do not know how long the son had been gone. It was long enough for him to spend a great deal of money, suffer through a famine, and hold down a job. Jesus did not give us a time frame. It was really irrelevant to His point. And yet it was part of the point. *Our heavenly Father's love is patient.* The story seems to indicate that the boy's father made it a habit of looking in the direction the boy had gone, hoping to see him returning. He was willing to restore his son no matter when he returned.

In the same way, your heavenly Father waits patiently for you when you leave for a season of sin. He does not sit and scheme about the things He will do to you once you return. Because He desires to have unbroken fellowship with you, He wants you to return. He wants you to take advantage of the depth of relationship He has made possible for you through Christ.

Patient but Eager

Third, *God is also eager to express His love.* Jesus made this clear when He said, "But while he was still a long way off, his father saw him, and felt compassion for him, and ran and embraced him, and kissed him" (Luke 15:20). In New Testament times no one who had any dignity ran in public. But when the father saw the son coming down the road, he ran.

This detail must have stunned the scribes and Pharisees. "God, eager to restore fellowship with sinners? How could this Jesus be so brazen as to portray the God of the universe running to a sinner and throwing His arms around him?" That was not the way they imagined God at all. They saw Him as a God who delighted in chastising sinners.

Do you realize that God is more eager to reestablish fellowship after you sin than you are? You can be assured of that by looking at what He did to make fellowship with Him possible to begin with. He can't wait for you to turn back to Him.

God is not sitting on His throne with a black notebook in one hand and a whip in the other waiting for you to return so that He can read off all you have done and chastise you for it. Like the father in the parable, He is eagerly waiting for you to return so He can restore you and clean you up. God's pardon is not miserly. Paul had this in mind when he wrote, "He who did not spare His own Son, but delivered Him up for us all, how will He not also with Him freely give us all things?" (Rom. 8:32).

THE FOCUS OF THE FATHER

A fourth facet of God the Father's attitude is that *His focus is on the sinner*, not the sin. Upon returning, the son immediately began to recite his prepared speech: "Father, I have sinned against heaven and in your sight; I am no longer worthy to be called your son" (Luke 15:21). His focus, like ours, was on his sin, his unworthiness. In essence he was begging for mercy. He readily acknowledged his father's right to reject his request for charity. He knew what he deserved, and he was willing to take what was coming.

The father, however, had an entirely different focus; his focus was on his son. The father seemingly ignored his son's speech. He began shouting orders to everyone:

> Quickly bring out the best robe and put it on him, and put a ring on his hand and sandals on his feet; and bring the fattened calf, kill it, and let us eat and be merry. (Luke 15:22–23)

"But what about the son's sin? What about all the money he wasted? What about the embarrassment he caused the family?" we may ask. Those were not the father's concerns. He had one thing, and one thing only, on his mind: "For this son of mine was dead, and has come to life again; he was lost, and has been found" (Luke 15:24).

God has dealt with your sin. It is no longer His focus. *You* are His focus. To God, your sin is no longer a hindrance to His fellowship with you. It is a hindrance only as long as you allow the guilt that accompanies sin to blind you to the fact that God is eager to reestablish fellowship with you. (We will deal more with this and the place of confession in the next chapter.)

Once you turn back to God, He is eager to take you back immediately. What you have done or how long you have done it is never a consideration. The father in the parable did not know what had happened to his son, where he had been, or how he had lost his money. And he did not ask. His son was back, and that was the only thing that mattered.

A JOYFUL WELCOME

We need to consider a fifth and final facet of God's attitude toward returning sinners. This one gives us great insight into the heart of God. *God receives the sinner back into fellowship joyfully.*

We see this in two statements Jesus made. First, He said, "But while he was still a long way off, his father saw him, and felt compassion for him" (Luke 15:20). Think about this. Jesus portrayed the heavenly Father in such a way that His immediate response to a returning sinner was compassion. Not anger, not frustration, not indignation—all of which we might think He would have been justified in feeling—but compassion.

When we are confronted with people who have hurt us or abused our relationship with them, our initial response—the one that just happens without our planning it—is usually anger or hurt. Then if we are really "spiritual," we may try to deal with those emotions by asking God to help us see things from His perspective. In time we can usually relate to those individuals in a civilized manner without blowing up and telling them how we feel.

That is what makes the father's first emotional response even more amazing to us. Out of his compassion he identified with the hurt and misery of his son, and he wanted to alleviate that pain. His own hurt did not get in the way of his ability to identify with his son's hurt.

So it is with the heavenly Father when you return to Him from your sin. He has dealt with the personal hurt sin caused Him. His focus is not on your hurt. Alleviating your pain and sorrow results in joy on His behalf.

We also see this idea of joy in Jesus' statement: "And they began to be merry" (Luke 15:24). It was a time of celebration for the father, and he threw a big party. His greatest desire had been fulfilled; his son had come home.

Jesus underscored this element of joy in each of the two parables preceding this one. When the shepherd found the lost sheep, he said, "Rejoice with me, for I have found my sheep which was lost!" (Luke 15:6). And then concerning the woman who lost her coin, "And when she has found it, she calls together her friends and neighbors, saying, 'Rejoice with me, for I have found the coin which I had lost!' (Luke 15:9). Jesus then summed up both parables by saying, "In the same way, I tell you, there is joy in the presence of the angels of God over one sinner who repents" (Luke 15:10).

When you or any child of God turns from sin, God rejoices. If it is possible to assign emotions to the heavenly Father, He "feels" compassion for you and therefore experiences joy at your homecoming. He does not wrestle with feelings of hurt and jealously. He has dealt with that once and for all. Instead,

He identifies with your hurt and frustration and takes joy in seeing you set free.

Accept God's True Character

I imagine it was difficult for many of those listening to Jesus to change their thinking about God and His attitude toward sinners. Those who did, however, opened themselves to lives of fellowship with their heavenly Father that had been unknown to them until that time. Those who refused to listen or who were too overwhelmed to believe remained in bondage to pride or despair. What about you? Are you willing to accept what Christ said about your heavenly Father? Are you willing to allow God to tear down the barriers that keep you from accepting Him as He really is?

You have a forgiving Father whose love and patience are unlimited. You cannot push Him too far. He is eager to have fellowship with you. You have a heavenly Father who is free to identify with your situation and who takes great joy in seeing you restored to your rightful place as His child. Your forgiving Father's greatest concern is *you*, not your sin. His focus is on you and your willingness to comply with His will for your life.

For some of you, this may come easy. For others, it may take some time to change your attitude about who God is and how He perceives you. Begin renewing your mind by thinking about these five tremendous facts about the character of God. To a great extent, they summarize everything we have discussed so far, and these principles come alive in the parable as we see them acted out in the response of the father toward his rebellious younger son.

A good way to start would be to recite this simple prayer

that incorporates all that we have seen about the character of God in this chapter.

Heavenly Father,
Sometimes it is difficult for me to see You as You really are.
By faith in the testimony of Jesus, however, I accept you as
  my forgiving heavenly Father.
A Father who loves me with unlimited love.
A Father whose patience is inexhaustible.
A Father who is eager to have fellowship with me.
A Father who focuses on me and my position as Your child, not
  on my sin.
A Father who rejoices when I turn to You from my sin
  whether it be one single act or a season of rebellion.
Expose the errors in my thinking toward You and fill me
  with the truth, for I know that in discovering the truth I
  will be set free. Amen.

QUESTIONS FOR PERSONAL GROWTH

1. What feelings do you have when you think about your earthly father? (Do you have feelings of love and acceptance or feelings of fear, dread, hurt, and disappointment?) How do you picture God the Father?

2. What two mind-sets polarized the Jews of Jesus' day?

3. What five aspects of God's attitude toward returning sinners are revealed in Jesus' parable of the lost son (Luke 15:11–24)?

4. Are you willing to accept what Christ said about your heavenly Father?

Six

FORGIVENESS AND CONFESSION

Now that we have examined God's part in forgiveness, what about our responsibility? You may be asking at this point, "Do we even have a responsibility? It sounds as if God has taken care of the whole thing from beginning to end." Remember, however, that the parable of the prodigal son portrays not only a forgiving father, but also a returning son. What about him?

The Scripture reads,

> But when he came to his senses, he said, "How many of my father's hired men have more than enough bread, but I am dying here with hunger! I will get up and go to my father, and will say to him, 'Father, I have sinned against heaven, and in your sight; I am no longer worthy to be called your son; make me one of your hired men.'" And he got up and came to his father. (Luke 15:17–20)

Out of a spirit of futility, hopelessness, and humility he made a decision to return to his father. Notice that he rehearsed what he would say: "I have sinned against heaven, and in your sight; I am no longer worthy to be called your son." And upon falling into his father's arms, he confessed just that: "I have sinned against heaven and in your sight; I am no longer worthy to be called your son." He confessed his sin to his father.

THE FATHER AND CONFESSION

It is vital to note that before the prodigal could confess his failure to his father, "his father saw him, and felt compassion for him, and ran and embraced him, and kissed him." The son's acceptance and forgiveness were not conditional upon his confession. As we discussed in the last chapter, the father was not motivated to forgive based on his son's confession of a life of sin. He fell into the arms of a father whose forgiveness was constant from the moment he walked away.

CONFESSION AND FORGIVENESS

Then why does the Bible teach that we are to confess our sins if we are already forgiven? What is the role of confession? If we are already forgiven, it seems unnecessary, doesn't it? The purpose of this chapter is to clarify the place of confession in God's strategy for our forgiveness.

The Greek word we use for *confess* means "to agree with." When we confess our sins to our heavenly Father, we are agreeing with Him. We are agreeing with His attitude about sin; that is, sin is against Him, it is destructive to His purpose for our lives, and it carries with it consequences that will prove painful.

Confession also implies that we are assuming responsibility

for our actions. We are not blaming our actions on others. Confession means that we see ourselves in relationship to our deeds of sin just as God does.

FIRST JOHN 1:9

Undoubtedly the most often-quoted verse regarding confession is this one: "If we confess our sins, He is faithful and righteous to forgive us our sins and to cleanse us from all unrighteousness" (1 John 1:9). When taken at face value, the verse would seem to indicate that our forgiveness is conditional upon our confession. This raises all kinds of questions: What if we forget to confess a sin? What if we don't realize we have committed a sin? And on and on we could go.

All of a sudden we have lost sight of what Christ has done on the cross, and we are focusing our attention on our memory and our sensitivity to sin. And if eternal life were dependent upon our ability to remember our sins, we would be correct in doing so. But there is a concept that will help us harmonize this verse with verses such as Ephesians 1:7, which says, "In Him we have [present tense] redemption through His blood, the forgiveness of our trespasses, according to the riches of His grace."

According to 1 John 1:9, we would expect Ephesians 1:7 to read: ". . . the forgiveness of our trespasses, according to the confession of our sins." So which is it? Are our sins forgiven based on His grace and the death of Christ two thousand years ago, or our up-to-the-minute confession?

Before I demonstrate how these two apparently conflicting ideas fit together, I want to reemphasize what I have said so far. The basis of our forgiveness is not confession, repentance, or faith, though all three are essential to our experience of forgiveness. The basis of our forgiveness is the sacrificial, sub-stitutionary death of Jesus Christ on the cross. His death as the sinless Son of God paid in full the penalty for all our sins—past, present, and future. We can add nothing to Christ's death that will gain for us any more forgiveness than we already have. That forgiveness becomes a reality in the life of every person who by faith receives Christ as Savior.

After we are saved, the basis of our continuing forgiveness is still none other than the shed blood of Christ at Calvary. Yet many believe that all future forgiveness is conditional upon the proper confession of sins. The basis of this thinking is under-standable upon reading 1 John 1:9. The first phrase in the verse sets up a condition that leads to confusion: "If we confess . . ."

One reason our forgiveness, insofar as our salvation is con-cerned, cannot be based upon our confession is that we are not always aware of our sins. In a hurried, insensitive moment, with a sharp word we can deeply hurt someone but be unaware of the damage to the person's spirit. In fact only God knows the real depth of our unrighteousness. He has made gracious and adequate provision for such actions. John assures us, "But if we walk in the light as He Himself is in the light, we have fellowship with one another, and the blood of Jesus His Son cleanses us from all sin" (1 John 1:7). Again, our forgiveness is inseparably connected with the blood Christ shed for us.

A FAMILY AFFAIR

The confusion over confession hinges on our tendency to assign certain definitions to words without regard to the con-text in which they are used. For instance, whenever we read the word *saved* in the Bible, we immediately think about eter-nal salvation from the penalty of our sins. And certainly the term *saved* is used that way. But not every time. For instance, when Jesus was hanging on the cross, one of the thieves hanging with Him shouted out, "*Save* Yourself and us!" (Luke 23:39). Clearly this was not a plea for salvation in the eternal sense. He just wanted Jesus to save his physical life. In Acts 27:20 Luke describes Paul's shipwreck, "And since neither sun nor stars appeared for many days, and no small storm was assailing us, from then on all hope of our being *saved* was gradually abandoned (emphasis mine)." Did Luke believe that since the storm was so bad they would all die and go to hell? Certainly not. Once again, *saved* refers to physical deliverance.

When we come to the concept of forgiveness, we must be careful not to assume that the author is always talking about the forgiveness a believer experiences when he or she first puts trust in Christ. Forgiveness in that sense is the door leading to a relationship with God. That type of forgiveness is a one-time-only phenomenon. Once pardoned, always pardoned.

The individual who becomes a child of God, thus establishing an eternal relationship with the heavenly Father, begins to relate to God in a new way. The new believer has new rights as well as new responsibilities. After the individual has become a partaker of eternal life, a new set of guidelines governs the relationship with God. One of these new guidelines has to do with restoring fellowship with the heavenly Father after the believer sins. The believer must receive what one author has termed "familial forgiveness."

Eternal salvation and forgiveness of the debt of sin separating us from God are not the issues here. This is a matter of family business. So John includes himself when he writes, "If *we* confess *our* sins." The parable of the prodigal son is the perfect illustration of this type of confession. The son's fellowship with his father could not have been restored until he first returned home. So it is with us. Until we turn back to God from our sin, fellowship is broken. Notice that God does not withhold fellowship; we, as sinning believers, damage the relationship. The following example may help to clarify this point.

THE CASE OF THE STOLEN WATCH

Suppose that just before I begin to preach I take off my watch and lay it on the pulpit. I forget that it is there and walk off and leave it. Someone from the balcony notices that I left it. He makes his way down to the platform area, and thinking that he is unobserved, he simply walks by the pulpit and slips the watch into his pocket.

However, someone sees him take my watch and the next day informs me as to the identity of the thief. It is someone I know. Naturally, I am surprised and disappointed, but I choose to forgive him. Once I deal with any negative feelings I may have, there is no barrier in my relationship with this man as far as I am concerned. My relationship with him has not changed. Even though he stole my only watch, I have forgiven him for his actions; I have canceled the debt; I have assumed the loss. When I see him sitting in the balcony the following Sunday, I do not say, "Hey, you stole my watch." I have forgiven him, so I must trust the Lord to convict him of his sin.

But suppose the offender discovers that I am aware of his action. By coincidence, we meet in the hallway. There are just the two of us, and I say to him, "How are you? I'm glad to see you." You see, I am free because I have forgiven him. I am not carrying the excess emotional weight of an unforgiving spirit, bitterness, or resentment for his action. But what do you suppose is going on inside him? He feels guilty, embarrassed, ashamed, fearful, regretful, found out.

I give him a warm, friendly handshake; I smile; I even invite him to lunch. But he nervously excuses himself; his eyes are unable to meet mine. He hurries off. He is miserable. His conscience is gnawing at him. His smile and sense of humor are gone.

The only way he is going to be comfortable around me and have fellowship with me again is to clear his conscience by confessing to me that he took my watch and by asking for my forgiveness.

My reply would then be, "You were already forgiven. I forgave you even before I knew who took it."

He did not have to come to me to get forgiveness; he was already forgiven. His confession was necessary for him to clear his conscience and to be restored to his previous fellowship with me.

That is what happens when we come to God confessing our sins. The confession does not persuade God to forgive us. He did that at the cross. The confession restores us to our previous level of fellowship and intimacy with Him—from our perspective. God did not change. He did not turn away from us because of our sins. His love was not affected. He was not disappointed. He already knows about the sins we are yet to commit, and His response is the same: "Forgiven!"

AND THE CONSEQUENCES?

I do not mean to imply that forgiven sins have no consequences. One scriptural principle does not nullify another. We are clearly warned, "Be sure your sin will find you out" (Num. 32:23). Sins may find us out only in our own conscience, or it could be a public discovery. But find us out they will. The apostle Paul warns us, "Do not be deceived, God is not mocked; for whatever a man sows, this he will also reap"

(Gal. 6:7). We may not reap it immediately nor in the way we expect, but we will reap.

Does this mean we are not forgiven? No! Then why do we have to suffer if God has forgiven us? There are two reasons. First, sin, by its very nature, is always accompanied by certain painful consequences, and the sin itself determines the nature of the consequences. It does not matter if we are saints or sinners. There are unavoidable consequences. That is the law of life.

For example, imagine a boy who has been instructed by his mother not to go into the street. He disobeys and runs out into the street. A car comes around the corner and hits the little boy. Does the mother forgive her son for disobeying? Absolutely. Even if he never asks for forgiveness. In fact forgiveness is not on her mind as she kneels down and holds his head in her lap. But in his forgiven state, the boy still suffers the pain and possible handicap of disobedience.

A second reason we must suffer the consequences is that God, though forgiving, is committed to conforming us to the image of His Son (Rom. 8:29). The painful consequences of our sins are expressions of God's love, not of His anger. He knows that to allow us to escape would only result in our continued disobedience and our ultimate failure. He reminds us, "For those whom the Lord loves He disciplines" (Heb. 12:6). He further encourages us by reminding us that "all discipline for the moment seems not to be joyful, but sorrowful; yet to those who have been trained by it, afterwards it yields the peaceful fruit of righteousness" (Heb. 12:11).

Confession is essential, not to receive forgiveness, but to experience the forgiveness God has provided through the death of Christ and to have unhindered fellowship with Him. But there is more. In confession we experience release from guilt, tension, pressure, and emotional stress resulting from our sins. Failure to confess our sins ensures the continuation of those unnecessary negative feelings.

THE POSITION OF BELIEVERS

I have been in small prayer groups where people began to confess their sins aloud. Often I have been tempted to stop them in the midst of their confession so that I can explain the proper way to confess sins to the heavenly Father. They cry out, "Oh, God, forgive me. Please forgive me, Lord. Oh, God, I beg of You to forgive me. I know I don't deserve it. Oh, Lord, what can I do to be forgiven? Oh, Lord, if You will just forgive me this time, I promise I will never do it again. Lord, if You will just give me one more chance, if You will forgive me just one more time." Sometimes it is evident from the increase in volume that they believe that if they pray a little louder, God may be a little more impressed and therefore respond a little more quickly.

I do not mean to be critical of another Christian's prayer for forgiveness. Heavy conviction by the Holy Spirit will often evoke great emotion and feelings of unworthiness and humiliation before the Lord. Yet demonstrations of emotion, long, loud prayers, and even fasting will not make things any better between the believer and God; only the simple, sincere confession of wrongdoing can do that. The blood of Christ provides for forgiveness, and confession is the avenue by which the believer experiences it.

Failure to understand the purpose and place of confession can result in fear and uncertainty about our salvation; it takes the cutting edge off our joy; it leaves us with a nagging doubt that deprives us of the peace our Lord intends for His children. We must remember that confession does not merit us any more love or forgiveness than we already have. "He who did not spare His own Son, but delivered Him up for us all, how will He not also with Him freely give us all things?" (Rom. 8:32).

If we are not clear about the nature and power of our confession, our service for Him will be hindered. Our ambivalence will short-circuit our motivation to serve God because we will not feel worthy or competent. We will have a nagging sense of guilt: *I wonder what God thinks of me? I wonder if He is pleased with me?* The cloud of doubt will continually hang over us: *Have I confessed everything? Am I sorry enough for my sins? Have I said the right thing?* When we understand our true position in Christ, these thoughts will no longer harass us. We will be able to confess our sins and, on the basis of Christ's shed blood, accept our forgiveness and thank God for His great grace toward us. And if some form of restitution needs to be made toward an offended party, we will do so.

Christ paid our penalty at Calvary. We cannot add to the payment by feeling sorry for our sins or confessing the same sin over and over again. This is not to belittle the awfulness of sin but to magnify the grace of God. Believers are united to Christ by faith. The following verses proclaim our position in Him:

There is therefore now no condemnation for those who are in Christ Jesus. (Rom. 8:1)

For He delivered us from the domain of darkness, and transferred us to the kingdom of His beloved Son, in whom we have redemption, the forgiveness of sins. (Col. 1:13–14)

In Him, you also, after listening to the message of truth, the gospel of your salvation—having also believed, you were sealed in Him with the Holy Spirit of promise, who is given as a pledge of our inheritance, with a view to the redemption of God's own possession, to the praise of His glory. (Eph. 1:13–14)

Who shall separate us from the love of Christ? . . . I am convinced that neither death, nor life, nor angels, nor principalities, nor things present, nor things to come, nor powers, nor height, nor depth, nor any other created thing, shall be able to separate us from the love of God, which is in Christ Jesus our Lord. (Rom. 8:35, 38–39)

Hallelujah! We are eternally secure in Christ. Failure to confess our sins does not alter our eternal security, but it interferes with, and greatly hinders, our fellowship with the Father. That is indeed a costly mistake.

WE'VE GOT TO BELIEVE IT

A primary reason we have no joy following our confession is that we do not really believe God has forgiven us. We think, *How could God forgive me? What I have done is awful.* We remain under a load of guilt we refuse to lay down because of our unbelief. I saw this principle work its way out in my relationship with one of my church members.

Alex was one of my best friends. His business was suffering, and he needed a short-term loan. I loaned him what he needed, which, by the way, was all I had and a rather sizable sum. Instead of investing it in his business, however, he paid off old bills. Suddenly, I didn't hear from him. He was not in his regular seat in the worship service. He avoided my calls.

Finally, through a mutual friend, I discovered that his business had folded. Still no contact. I was struggling with my own attitude of disappointment and hurt. Finally, I was able to say to the Lord, "I forgive him the debt. If he never pays me back, it's all right. I still love him as a friend."

After a period of time, we met. I told him that he was forgiven and that I did not expect him to repay me. I tried to communicate to him that he did not owe me anything and that I still wanted to be his friend.

But Alex could not accept my forgiveness. He became critical of me to others. Finally, he declared bankruptcy to prevent me from suing him, which I would never have considered. He ruined his credit rating, his reputation, his relationship to our church, and his usefulness to the Lord's work—all because he could not accept the full and free forgiveness of a friend who truly loved him. He could not believe that anyone would forgive him for misusing that much money. He is still out of fellowship with God and out of service for God. He carries an unnecessary load of guilt because he would not accept the gift of forgiveness.

So it is with believers if we will not let go of the guilt that always accompanies sin. We put ourselves through unnecessary trauma and pain. Often it affects the relationship with God and relationships with others as well.

BUT JESUS SAID . . .

In the Sermon on the Mount, Jesus made a statement about forgiveness that may appear to contradict much or all of what we have discussed in this chapter. He said,

> For if you forgive men for their transgressions, your heavenly Father will also forgive you. But if you do not forgive men, then your Father will not forgive your transgressions. (Matt. 6:14–15)

Does this mean that my failure to forgive someone who has wronged me will deprive me of the forgiveness God purchased in my behalf through Christ's blood at Calvary?

The answer to this question goes back to understanding what Christ meant by the word *forgive*. He was talking to God-fearing Jews, men and women who were seeking the truth about how they should relate to God. His statement must be interpreted in the context of family.

To forgive means to release others from a debt incurred when they wronged us. The debt may be material or emotional, some form of hurt or embarrassment. When we forgive, we assume the loss. We free others from the bondage of material or emotional indebtedness. If we refuse to forgive, we place ourselves in bondage to an unforgiving spirit, which is accompanied by tension, strife, pressure, irritation, frustration, and anxiety.

Therefore, because it is always the will of the Father for us to be forgiving toward others, refusing to forgive our offenders prevents God from releasing us from the same bondage. In love He cannot simply overlook our un-Christlike spirit; we must deal with it by confessing it and forgiving those who have offended us. Otherwise we bear the pressure of His chastisement, which is His refusal to release us from the natural penalty of an unforgiving spirit.

When Jesus says in this passage, "Then your Father will not forgive your transgressions," He is not implying that our salvation is in jeopardy. Our fellowship with Him is what will suffer. We cannot be right with God and unforgiving toward others. Confession is absolutely essential if we are to walk in fellowship with our heavenly Father, whose forgiveness toward us is eternal, whose unconditional love toward us cannot be diminished, and whose grace toward us can never be thwarted.

When you sin, what should you do? Thank Him at that moment for bringing your sin to your attention. Assume responsibility for it, agreeing with Him that you have sinned. Thank Him for His forgiveness purchased at Calvary through the blood of His Son. If the sin is against another person, make things right as soon as possible. Then go on with perfect confidence that things are right between you and your Creator.

Questions for Personal Growth

1. If your sins are already forgiven, why should you confess your sins?

2. What is the basis of continuing forgiveness?

3. How should you treat a person who has wronged you? What happens if you refuse to forgive someone who has wronged you?

4. Why is confession essential for believers?

Seven

HANDLING OUR HURTS

As a young man, Jim wanted to be a medical doctor. He studied hard all through elementary school and high school. His hard work paid off, and he graduated with excellent grades. But when the time came for him to go away to college, his father refused to allow him to leave. He forced him to stay on the family farm and work.

At the age of twenty-three, Jim had taken all he could take of farm life. He packed up his belongings, loaded his car, and left. Along with his clothes and a few books, he took something else with him as well. He drove away that day with a heart full of bitterness and resentment toward his father.

Everywhere Jim went he had a difficult time getting along with others. As people would try to get close to him, his bitterness would pour out all over them. He seemed unable to make long-lasting friendships, and he was filled with feelings of rejection and isolation. Consequently, he found himself moving from job to job; he was never able to settle down.

Finally, he met a woman who really cared for him. After a

short engagement, they were married. She was a widow with one son. Three weeks into the marriage an unexpected outburst of anger marked the beginning of over forty years of hell on earth for his loyal wife. His short temper and vile language drove away the few friends he had, and eventually, his wife's friends could no longer tolerate his behavior. Right up to the last days of his life—nearly blind, senile, and unable to care for himself—the poison of bitterness continued to eat away at Jim's heart. And all because he was unwilling to deal with the rejection and hurt he had experienced as a teenager.

I don't know all the reasons why Jim's father would not let him leave the farm. Maybe he was uneducated and was threatened by Jim's educational pursuits. He may have just been selfish and not wanted to lose Jim as a farmhand. Let's give him the benefit of the doubt and say he was justified in feeling hurt because of his father's decision. In spite of being "justified," however, Jim's reaction did not hurt his father half as badly as it hurt him. Such is the nature of an unforgiving spirit. It is like a hot coal. The longer and tighter it is held, the deeper the burn. Like a hot coal, bitterness too will leave a scar that even time cannot erase.

DEVELOPING AN UNFORGIVING SPIRIT

An unforgiving spirit does not develop overnight. It involves a process of responses and thus takes time to develop. In talking with people through the years I have discovered ten stages an individual is likely to go through. Not everyone will pass through each stage, but almost everyone I have known with an unforgiving spirit could identify with several of them.

We Get Hurt

The seeds of an unforgiving spirit are planted when we are wronged or hurt in some way. It could be a physical, an emotional, or a verbal hurt. It could be a hurt we experienced in childhood or adulthood. It really makes no difference. Since we live in such a self-centered world, often we experience our first hurt as a child, and unfortunately, this early hurt usually comes from the people we love and respect the most.

As we discussed in Chapter 1, all our hurts are really some form of rejection. We may not perceive it as rejection initially, but that is what happens when we are wronged by others. We may feel hurt, pain, abandonment, embarrassment, hatred, or some other negative emotion. But it all relates to rejection.

Feeling rejected, then, is the first stage in developing an unforgiving spirit. That being the case, we all have the potential for problems in this area. Therefore, we must always be on our guard to stop the process in its beginning stages.

We Become Confused

Often our initial response to hurt, regardless of the form it takes, is confusion. We experience a sense of bewilderment; we are not quite sure how to respond. It is similar to being in a state of shock. In this stage, we may think, *This is not really happening.* We may even have a physical reaction, such as a deep feeling of emptiness in the pit of the stomach. Many people have actually gotten sick after experiencing rejection. This stage is usually short-lived, and immediately, we move into the third stage.

We Look for Detours

We all have a desire to avoid pain. Because of that, when we are hurt emotionally, instead of thinking about it we need to find ways of avoiding those painful thoughts or memories. We take mental detours. We don't allow ourselves to think about certain things. We change the subject when certain topics are brought up. This desire to detour around past hurt motivates many people to drink heavily or to become addicted to both prescription and nonprescription drugs. The fact is, I have never counseled a drug addict or an alcoholic who was not trying to cover up the pain of the past. The root problem was never alcohol or drugs; it was always the inability to cope with rejection.

We also take physical detours. We tend to avoid certain people, places, and things. Anything that reminds us of the hurt becomes off-limits. I will never forget one preacher's daughter I counseled. She was full of bitterness toward her father. During our conversation, she made the statement, "I would never marry a preacher." There was certainly no real connection between her father and every prospective preacher in the world. But in her mind there was. Preacher meant "rejection." Therefore, preachers were to be avoided at all costs.

A college student in our church could not stand me, and I did not understand why. Finally, one of his friends explained. His father constantly quoted me, especially when he was disciplining his son. The young man's problem was really between him and his father. But since he had been hurt by his father, he looked with disdain upon anyone or anything associated with his father.

We Dig a Hole

After we try to "schedule" around our hurt, that is, to arrange our thought patterns and lives in general so as never to come into contact with anything that reminds us of our hurt (an undertaking that is rarely successful), we attempt to forget the whole thing ever occurred. We dig a hole and bury it as deeply as we can.

We Deny It

The fifth stage is also one of denial. We deny that we were ever hurt or that we are covering up anything. We smile and say, "Oh, I have dealt with that." Or "I forgave him long ago."

This is a tough stage for people to break out of. I have met score of adults who are carrying around a load of bitterness, as demonstrated through their tempers or other negative behavior, but they see no connection between a turbulent childhood and their problems as adults. One woman's problems were so obviously connected to her relationship with her father that everyone who knew anything about her past tried to get her to see the connection. She flatly denied it.

I know of a lost friend who recommended that a church member get counseling to deal with his bitterness toward his father. The church member, however, just laughed when confronted with the notion that his relationship with his father was in any way connected to his present struggles. "I was just a kid when all that happened," he said, referring to an incident in which he was clearly rejected by his father.

We Become Defeated

Regardless of how successfully we think we have buried our hurt, it will still work its way out through our behavior. A short temper, oversensitivity, shyness, a critical spirit, jealously—all of these can be evidence of unresolved rejection. The tragedy is that when we deny that we are harboring hurt, we will look everywhere but the right place for a way to change the resulting undesirable behavior. We can move, change jobs, change friends, rededicate our lives, make New Year's resolutions, memorize Scripture, pray long prayers, fast, or undertake any number of spiritual exercises. But until we deal with the root of the problem, we will ultimately be defeated in our attempts to change.

I see this in marriage counseling all the time. A wife will tell a horror story of how her husband (who is sitting right there) abuses her verbally and sometimes physically. She describes his violent and unpredictable temper in detail. She weeps as she gives account after account of how her husband has made her life and the lives of the kids unbearable.

Surprisingly enough, the husband in this situation often shakes his head in agreement with everything his wife has accused him of. I have seen husbands break down and cry in shame at the things they have done and the pain they have caused. Yet, more times than not, they walk out the door at the end of what seems like a "life-changing" counseling session and repeat the same contemptible behavior. Why? Because even though they may be sorry for their behavior, they have not dealt with the root problem.

On the other hand, I have seen men and women deal with the anger and hurt they have been carrying with them. I have seen men deal once and for all with their tempers. I have seen women lay down forever the unrealistic expectations they had of their husbands. The quick turnarounds always came about after the root of bitterness was discovered, acknowledged, and dealt with. (We will discuss in a later chapter how this is accomplished.)

We Become Discouraged

This is the critical stage. It is usually the stage where we either seek professional help or bail out of our present circumstances altogether. After a while it seems as if things will never change or never get any better. Any little bit or progress we may see is always shattered by another incident that just confirms the suspicion that it's hopeless!

This is the stage in which husbands leave their wives either because their wives will not change or because they are unable to rekindle that "loving feeling" they once had. This is the stage in which women begin to depend upon alcohol and prescription drugs to make it through the day.

An unforgiving spirit destroys respect. If allowed to go unchecked, it can dissolve the loyalty and even the sense of duty that are so necessary to hold a marriage together during difficult times. Extramarital affairs become a viable option to people who have publicly spoken out against adultery. Divorce becomes a real option to couples who pledged an unconditional lifetime of commitment. For those who can foresee no better circumstances in this life, they often choose to escape by taking their own lives. Such is the power and the poison of an unforgiving spirit.

We Discover the Truth

For some of us, there is a happy ending. Through someone's help or by God's grace, we discover the root of bitterness. We gain insight into why we act the way we do. We are able to see the connection between the past and the present. The pieces finally fit together.

We Take Responsibility

The ninth stage is closely associated with the eighth one. In this stage we own up to our responsibility. We decide to quit blaming others. We decide to quit waiting for everybody and everything else around us to change. W open our hearts for God to have His way, regardless of how it might hurt.

We Are Delivered

The final outcome for those of us who are willing to deal with an unforgiving spirit is deliverance. My friend, you can be free of that embarrassing, inappropriate, family-splitting behavior. You say, "But you don't know what has happened to me. You don't know what I have been through." You are right. But I have known people in all kinds of circumstances who have been delivered and restored.

SO WHAT ARE YOU WAITING FOR?

You may be using the excuse that your circumstances are so bad that you could never forgive the person or persons who hurt you. The fact is, however, that you could if you are willing to. If you are not willing to forgive, you will ultimately bring your own life crashing down around you. It will be nobody else's fault but your own.

If you are unwilling to forgive, you have one (or more) of several problems. First, your willingness could be a result of *selfishness*. You have been hurt. Something unfair has happened to you. You did not get your way. Your thoughts have turned inward, and you are concerned only with yourself, your rights, and your feelings. You are waiting for the world to come to you and ask forgiveness before you are willing to forgive. *After all*, you think, *it was that other person's fault*. You live in a prison made of your emotions and expectations. It is selfishness because you have the ability to do something about it if you choose. You just may be too selfish to make the first move.

Perhaps your problem is *pride*. When there is pride in a heart, it is very difficult to be forgiving. Pride steps into the forefront of your thinking and says, "Look what they have done to me. If I forgive them, people will think I am weak and I do not have any backbone."

Pride tells you to somehow get back at those who have hurt you. Harboring anger in your heart makes you feel as if you are getting revenge; in fact, it only destroys you. The real problem is that when you set out to get revenge—even if it is only in your mind—you are assuming a responsibility that has been given to Christ and Christ alone. He is the Judge. At the right time, those who have hurt you will pay the penalty for their sin (Rom. 14:10). In the meantime, you are to forgive.

A third reason you may not be willing to forgive is that you are struggling with *low self-esteem*. Let me explain how this works. People with low self-esteem feel insignificant to begin with. Often, without really understanding what is taking place, they will attach their significance to the wrong they suffered. I have met people who have lived most of their adult lives in response to a wrong they suffered at the hands of an unfair boss. They are constantly saying things like this: "You know I would not be here if it were not for . . . I could have gone far if I had not lost my job with . . ." The unfair circumstances become a point of reference for everything else in their lives.

When this happens to people, they cannot afford to forgive. To deal with the hurt they suffered would be to take away the thing most essential to their identity. They would no longer get the sympathy from others they have come to rely on. They would have no more sad stories to tell. They would have no more excuses for their lack of diligence and discipline.

Do you have a habit of always bringing up a particular event in your life when you were treated unfairly? To know for sure, ask your closest friends or your spouse. Without knowing it, you may have allowed your identity to become intertwined with an event you need to put behind you. Your true and eternal identity is found in your relationship with God through Christ. To experience the joy and freedom available to you in Christ, you must forgive those who have wronged you and move on.

Another reason you may be unwilling to deal with your unforgiving spirit is that *you think you already have*. Sometime in your past you may have acknowledged that you were wronged. You may have admitted that you "needed" to forgive others. You may have even prayed a prayer in which you said the words "I forgive _____." You may have meant it with all your heart, yet if there is evidence emotionally and verbally that something is still gnawing at you on the inside, if you are still uncomfortable around the people who wronged you or if things that remind you of them still make you become tense on the inside, chances are you have not completely dealt with the situation. In the next chapter we will deal with how to make forgiveness complete.

A fifth reason a person refuses to forgive is that it is *painful*. Being willing to forgive is painful in the sense that thinking about past hurts often brings back the original unpleasant emotions. Forgiveness can be especially painful if the wrong hurt so deeply that the pain suffered was buried and forgotten. The very thought of digging that back up, which is sometimes necessary, causes many people to run.

This is especially true of those who were hurt as children. Cases dealing with child abuse, incest, rape, severe beatings, or catching a parent in an extramarital affair are extremely painful. Sometimes these incidents have all but been erased from memory. Yet they are often the keys to complete healing and freedom. As I have talked to people about their pasts, looking for a clue to their struggles, often I will touch on a subject that brings immediate tears to their eyes. They say, "I can't talk about that" or "I would rather not go into all that." Usually, the doors they want to walk through least, they need to walk through most.

If you live with events in your past that are painful to even think about, please accept by faith that it is worth the pain in order to be set free. God wants to perform spiritual surgery. He wants to remove the bitterness and the hurt. It will hurt, but it will heal. And whatever scar may be left will be much easier to live with than the open wound you now bear.

There is one last reason: *You don't know how to be forgiving.* Maybe you are at the point of being able to say, "I am ready. Just tell me what to do." I hope so. For a long time I lived with the knowledge that I needed to forgive people in my past, but I did not know exactly what to do. The following chapters will help you understand the process of forgiveness and what you must do to be forgiving.

WHERE ARE YOU?

Before we go any further, I want you to think back over what I have said in this chapter. Have you been wronged or hurt recently or in your past? Was your tendency to try to forget about it, to move on to something or somebody else? Did you get into the habit of burying the painful emotions that seemed to raise their ugly heads time after time? Do you find yourself staying away from certain people or certain types of people? Are there places and things that cause you to feel the hurt all over again? Are there behavior patterns that you find impossible to change?

Are you wrestling with depression? Are you fighting the urge to just bust loose from your present circumstances because the pressure is too much to bear? Are you tired of hurting the people you love the most? Does the grass look greener some-where else? Are you beginning to wonder if your family and the world would not be better off without you?

If you answered yes to any of these questions, chances are there are some people you need to forgive. It could very well be that you are harboring an unforgiving spirit. Please don't allow your pride and selfishness to get in the way. Please don't allow your fear of the ensuing pain to stop you. You may be on the verge of a miracle in your life. You may be about to be set free.

QUESTIONS FOR PERSONAL GROWTH

1. Name and explain the ten stages of an unforgiving spirit.

2. Name six reasons why a person may refuse to forgive others.

3. Give an example of a time when you resisted forgiving another. How did you feel about God? Give an example of a time when you freely forgave another. How did you feel about God?

4. Are there some people you are unwilling to forgive? Think about how an unforgiving spirit has affected you.

Eight

FORGIVING OTHERS

When I think about God's grace and the depth of His healing power, I think about a wonderful woman I met through my son. Never before have I met a woman who has suffered so greatly and yet forgiven so deeply. Her story perfectly illustrates how the principles of forgiveness are applied to the particular circumstances of an individual.

When Jill first showed up at the counseling office, she was a very frightened woman. Sitting in a room with only an empty chair to talk to, she began a process that took her back thirty-one years to when she was twelve years old. (For more information about this process, see Appendix B.) That day, as though her uncle were sitting across from her, she began to talk to him about things that had transpired years ago . . . how he had taken advantage of her innocence and abused her time and time again. She told him of the hurt, the anger, and the hatred that she felt for so many years.

Then the tone of her voice changed . . . the bitterness gave way to understanding and the hate to words of forgiveness. "What you did to me as a child has been a factor in everything that has happened to me since then. How can I forgive you? I'll tell you how. I realized some time ago that I needed to ask someone to forgive me. That someone was God. And when I asked Him for forgiveness, this is what He said, 'Your sins were forgiven when My Son died on the cross. You are already forgiven. Accept it and begin to live your life as a daughter, not as a slave to your sin.' I realized that in the moment when Jesus died on the cross, I was forgiven for everything I would ever do! I just had to accept it. When I realized that God had forgiven me for everything I'd ever done or ever would do, I began to understand that I had no right *not* to forgive you. So today, I'm setting us both free from what happened such a long time ago. I forgive you."

With tears that began to wash away the bitterness, she went through a list of names. With each one, she went through the same process. She spoke of the pain that had consumed her for years. She talked about the rejection, the feeling that it really didn't matter to anyone if she lived or died. When she came to the last name on the list, she stopped, "How can I forgive you? I don't know if I can. Yet, I think if I don't, I won't ever be free." With that, she pictured herself in the chair. She talked about the things she'd done to prove how "bad" she was and to hurt herself. When she had said it all, she said one more time, "If God forgave me for everything I've ever done, what right have I not to forgive you?"

That day as she left the room she had forgiven the people in her past who had hurt her so deeply, and she had forgiven herself too. Because of that, she walked out a free person— free of the bitterness and hate that had made her a prisoner. It took thirty-one years to forgive the person she had blamed for having "such a miserable life," but it took only a couple of hours to discover the freedom that God has provided when someone learns what it is to forgive.

A PERSONAL MATTER

Forgiveness is something that each of us has had to deal with in one way or another. What might take you just a short time to work through might be a process that takes someone else time, prayer, and godly counsel. But it is a process we cannot ignore, not if we want to be free to become the persons God created us to be. If we refuse to deal with the bitterness and resentments that put us in bondage, we cannot have the fellowship with our Father that we are supposed to have.

In my years of being a minister and in counseling with people, I have talked with many people like Jill who have spent years in bondage to someone because they were either unable or unwilling to forgive that person. I have also seen the freedom they come to know when they finally understand and appropriate the idea of forgiveness.

In this chapter we will look at the practical aspects of learning how to forgive. But before we do, we need to get rid of some stumbling blocks to true forgiveness.

CLEARING UP SOME CONFUSION

One of the stumbling blocks to actually forgiving others is all the wrong information that has entered into our theology. Some of these ideas have crept in through the repeated use of clichés. Others have just been passed on from generation to generation with no biblical basis whatsoever.

The first idea we need to clear up is this: Is justifying, understanding, or explaining away someone's behavior the same as forgiving him? I can certainly understand that "my brother" was under a lot of stress when he raised his voice to me in front of my customers, but does that mean I have forgiven him?

Certainly not. Understanding someone's situation is part of the forgiveness process, but only a part.

Another mistaken idea we have picked up is that time heals all wounds. I think that is one of the most misused (and damaging) clichés I've heard. How could the passage of time or the process of forgetting lead to forgiveness? How many times have we said that to someone with good intentions? It was thirty-one years later that Jill forgave her uncle. If time were the healing factor, certainly the hurt she experienced would have been taken care of long before she walked into the counseling office. Yet she admitted that time only made things worse.

Here is another misunderstanding that I have already touched on briefly: Is forgiving others *denying* that we have been hurt or pretending that the hurt was no big deal? We may try to convince ourselves (after forgiving others) that what they did really wasn't such a big thing, after all. This form of denial works against the forgiveness process. It's denying that others hurt us in a way that caused us real physical, mental, or emotional pain. It's like denying a real part of ourselves.

Another misconception says that to forgive others, we must go to them personally and confess our forgiveness. Confessing our forgiveness to someone who has not first solicited our forgiveness usually causes more problems than it solves. I will never forget the young man in our church who asked one of the women on our staff to forgive him for lusting after her. She had no idea he had a problem with lust, and his confession caused her to be embarrassed and self-conscious around him from then on.

I rarely counsel people to confess their forgiveness to those who have hurt them if the other persons have not asked for it. Once we begin to understand the nature of forgiveness, it becomes clear why this principle holds true. God forgave us long before we ever asked for it. As we have seen,

He has forgiven us of things we will never ask forgiveness for. In the same way, we are free to forgive others of things they will never know about.

I say *rarely* because there are some occasions when confession of this type is appropriate. Keep in mind that there is a difference between telling others you have forgiven them and actually forgiving them. Forgiving others should begin at the time you are offended, whereas actually confessing our forgiveness may take place later. We need not wait until a person asks for forgiveness to do so. If that were true, many times we would wait forever.

We should confess our forgiveness if one of two situations occurs. First, we should confess our forgiveness if asked for it. This helps clear the other person's conscience and assures them that we do not hold anything against them.

Second, we should confess our forgiveness if we feel the Lord would have us confront others about their sin. Their sin may have been directed against us personally or against someone we love. It may be necessary in the course of conversation to assure them that you have forgiven them and are coming more for their sake than your own. When we confront others about their sin, the issue of forgiveness must be settled in our own hearts. We must never confront in order to force another to ask for our forgiveness.

Forgiveness is a much more involved issue than just putting time between us and the event or saying some words in a prayer. It is a process that involves understanding our own forgiveness and how that applies to those who have hurt us.

FORGIVING OTHERS

Forgiveness is an act of the will that involves five steps.

We Are Forgiven

First, we must recognize that *we have been totally forgiven.* Most people get hung up on this point. That is the reason I have explained in such detail the foundation for forgiveness. Paul sums it all up beautifully: "For the death that He died, He died to sin, once for all; but the life that He lives, He lives to God" (Rom. 6:10).

Once we understand the depth of our sin and the distance it put between us and God, and once we get a glimpse of the sacrifice God made to restore fellowship with us, we should not hesitate to get involved in the process of forgiveness. To understand what God did for us and then to refuse to forgive those who have wronged us is to be like the wicked, ungrateful slave Jesus described:

> For this reason the kingdom of heaven may be compared to a certain king who wished to settle accounts with his slaves. And when he had begun to settle them, there was brought to him one who owed him ten thousand talents. But since he did not have the means to repay, his lord commanded him to be sold, along with his wife and children and all that he had, and repayment to be made. The slave therefore falling down, prostrated himself before him, saying, "Have patience with me, and I will repay you everything." And the lord of that slave felt compassion and released him and forgave him the debt.
>
> But that slave went out and found one of his fellow slaves who owed him a hundred denarii; and he seized him and began to choke him, saying, "Pay back what you owe." So his fellow slave fell down and began to entreat him, saying, "Have patience with me and I will repay you." He was unwilling however, but went and threw him in prison until he should pay back what was owed. So when his fellow slaves saw what

had happened, they were deeply grieved and came and reported to their lord all that had happened.

Then summoning him, his lord said to him, "You wicked slave, I forgave you all that debt because you entreated me. Should you not also have had mercy on your fellow slave, even as I had mercy on you?" And his lord, moved with anger, handed him over to the torturers until he should repay all that was owed him. (Matt. 18:23–34)

We read the parable and think, *How could anyone be so ungrateful?* But the believer who will not forgive another is even more guilty and more ungrateful than that slave. The first step, then, is to realize that we have been totally forgiven of a debt we could never pay and thus have no grounds for refusing to forgive others.

Forgive the Debt

The second step is to *release the person from the debt* we think is owed us for the offense. This must be a mental, an emotional, and sometimes even a physical release. It involves mentally bundling up all our hostile feelings and surrendering them to Christ.

We can accomplish this in one of two ways: either by meeting face-to-face or, as Jill did, by using a substitute. Both work equally well, but one may be more appropriate than the other. In cases where a person is dead, lives far away, or is totally unapproachable, it will be necessary to use the chair-substitute method.

Accept Others

The third step is to *accept others as they are* and release them from any responsibility to meet our needs. I am sure we have all met people who have placed the responsibility for their acceptability on us or someone we know. You may be like that yourself. Certain people can make or break your day depending on the amount of attention they pay you. This is a common trait in people who are unable or unwilling to forgive. But when we decide as an act of the will to forgive, we absolve others of any responsibility to meet our needs.

View Others as Tools of Growth

Fourth, we must *view those we have forgiven as tools in our lives* to aid us in our growth in and understanding of the grace of God. Even with all my Bible knowledge and education, cannot understand and appreciate the grace of God as Jill can. Though she would not go through what she has been through again for a million dollars, neither would she take a million for what she has learned about her heavenly Father.

Joseph certainly understood this principle. After all his brothers did to him, he was able to forgive them. He saw them as the instruments of God to get him to Egypt and to be in such a position of power that he could save his family when the famine destroyed all the crops. So when his brothers fell down before him, fearful of what he might do to them to get even, he said,

Do not be afraid, for am I in God's place? And as for you [speaking of his brothers], you meant evil against me, but God meant it for good in order to bring about this present result, to preserve many people alive. So therefore, do not be afraid; I will provide for you and your little ones. (Gen. 50:19–21)

Make Reconciliation

The last thing we must do is to *make reconciliation* with those from whom we have been estranged. This will vary from situation to situation. But if there is a family member, distant relative, former employee, or maybe an ex-friend we have avoided because we had hostility in our hearts against that person, we need to reestablish contact. We may have to begin by apologizing. Regardless of how we go about it, we must do what we can to restore fellowship with those who hurt us. Once our forgiveness is complete, reconciliation will be much easier. In fact, many people I have counseled have rushed back to estranged friends and relatives to reestablish contact. Once the barrier of unforgiveness is removed, all the old pleasant feelings can surface, and there is actually joy in the process of restoration.

After completing the five steps in forgiveness, we should pray this simple prayer:

> *Lord, I forgive (name of person) for (name the specifics). I take authority over the Enemy, and in the name of Jesus Christ and by the power of His Holy Spirit, I take back the ground I have allowed Satan to gain in my life because of my attitude toward (the person) and give this ground back to my Lord Jesus Christ.*

We don't have to pray this prayer word for word, but it is a suggested model to use when dealing with forgiving someone. It is essential to name the person and what is being forgiven.

WHAT IF IT HAPPENS AGAIN?

What if the one we have forgiven hurts us again? What if the very same thing happens again? Will it make what we've done any less real? At first we will no doubt feel hurt, bitter, or angry—or maybe all three. Satan will remind us of our past hurts. We may be tempted to doubt the sincerity of our decision to forgive that person.

If this happens, it is important to remember that forgiveness is an act of the will. The initial decision to forgive the person must be followed by the faith walk of forgiveness. Standing firm on the decision to forgive that person and applying additional forgiveness, if necessary, allow us to replace the hurt and the defeated memories with faith victories. The new offenses can be forgiven as they occur without linking them to past offenses, which have already been forgiven.

It is equally important to remember that forgiveness is for our benefit. The other person's behavior may never change. It is up to God, not us, to change that person. It is our responsibility to be set free from the pressure and weight of an unforgiving attitude.

WE WILL KNOW WE HAVE FORGIVEN WHEN . . .

Several things will occur once the forgiveness process is complete. First, our negative feelings will disappear. We will not feel the way we used to feel when we run into these people on the street or in the office. Harsh feelings may be replaced by feelings of concern, pity, or empathy, but not resentment.

Second, we will find it much easier to accept the people who have hurt us without feeling the need to change them; we will be willing to take them just the way they are. We will have a new appreciation for their situation once the blinders of resentment have been removed from our eyes. We will understand more why they acted and continue to act the way they do.

Third, our concern about the needs of the other individuals

will outweigh our concerns about what they did to us. We will be able to concentrate on them, not on ourselves or our needs.

Forgiveness is a process that can be painful and at times seem unending. Whatever our pain, whatever our situation, we cannot afford to hold on to an unforgiving spirit another day. We must get involved with the process of forgiving others and find out what it means to be really free. If we will persevere and keep our eyes on the One who forgave us, it will be a liberating force like nothing else we have ever experienced.

Questions for Personal Growth

1. Identify and discuss four common misconceptions about forgiveness.

2. Forgiveness is an act of will that involves five steps. Name and explain these five steps.

3. If people hurt you repeatedly, what should you do? Should you try to change their behavior? Why or why not? What three things can you expect to happen once the forgiveness process is complete?

4. Can you recall experiencing these results?

Nine

FORGIVING OURSELVES

Forgiveness is based on the atoning work of the Cross, and not on anything we do. God's forgiveness does not depend on our confession, nor does His fellowship. Confession is a means for releasing us from the tension and bondage of a guilty conscience. When we pray, *God, You are right. I've sinned against You. I am guilty of this act. I am guilty of that thought,* we achieve release.

Our fellowship with God is not restored by confession (because it was never broken); rather, our sense of fellowship with God is restored. When we sin, we withdraw our fellowship from God; He does not withdraw His fellowship from us. Forgiveness is ours forever as believers. The moment we received Him as Savior, He became our life. But our capacity to enjoy forgiveness—our capacity to enjoy a clean conscience—is based on our willingness to acknowledge and confess that sin.

Let me illustrate. One night when I came home, instead of driving into the garage as is my habit, I pulled in the side parking area. As I was walking toward the back door, I noticed my almost-new Oldsmobile sitting there—with the front end bashed in. My daughter, Becky, had been driving the car. I decided not to mention it. When I entered the house, nothing was said. When we sat down to dinner, nothing was said. After a while, my son Andy said, "Becky, do you have anything you'd like to tell Dad?"

I noticed that Becky was quiet. She hadn't said much that night. She turned to me and said, "Dad, oh, I hate to tell you this." She was having a terrible time, "I want to tell you what happened. This fellow pulled in front of me and he stopped all of a sudden and I ran into him and I bashed up your car." And she started crying.

I didn't say a word until she was finished. Then, "Becky, it's okay. It's all right."

"You mean you're not mad?"

"Why should I be mad? You're not hurt. You can always have the car fixed up again. Even if it were your fault, Becky, it's okay."

Becky is my daughter. If she had totaled the car and we had not had insurance, she would have been just as forgiven. She's my daughter, and as my daughter, she walks in total forgiveness by me—no matter what she does. Even so, Becky had to clear her conscience that night. She had to get it out of her system and tell me about it, or she would have spent a miserable night trying to sleep. And she had to forgive herself.

Isn't this what happens with us and God?

Forgiveness is never complete until, first, we have experienced the forgiveness of God; second, we can forgive others who have wronged us; and third, we are able to forgive ourselves.

People frequently say, "I know that God has forgiven me. And I'm sure that I have forgiven those who wronged me.

But I still have no peace in my heart. Something is not quite right." Oftentimes this disquietude can be an unforgiving spirit directed toward others for what they have done. There will be no peace in our hearts until we forgive ourselves for the wrongs that we have committed. *But we must be willing to forgive ourselves.*

Not long ago, a young woman, whom I shall call Patsy, came to see me. She was only sixteen, but she had become sexually involved with an eighteen-year-old when she was thirteen. This had continued for two years before he moved to another state. She called herself "dirty and guilty." Distraught by his departure, overwhelmed by her sense of guilt, and reluctant to talk to her parents, she sought private counseling—only to become emotionally involved with the thirty-year-old counselor on whom she had depended for help.

By the time Patsy came to see me, she was confused and desperate. She had thought about running away from home and had toyed with the idea of suicide. She didn't know what to do or where to turn. She said, "I know that I'm saved, but I'm so full of guilt I don't know what in the world to do. And if, somehow, I don't get an answer, I know I can't keep living."

"Have you asked the Lord Jesus Christ to forgive you?"

"I've asked Him hundreds of times to forgive me."

"Well, has He?" She didn't answer.

"Well, has He forgiven you?"

"I feel so dirty."

"But, did you ask Him to forgive you?"

"Oh, I've asked Him many times."

"How did He respond?"

"I just feel so dirty inside," she repeated.

Because of her testimony, I believe that Patsy was saved.

But what she did was so sinful and wicked and vile in her eyes that she could not believe a holy God could forgive her for two years of sexual immorality with one man and almost another year of intimate involvement with another. Patsy said she just couldn't "feel" God's forgiveness.

Patsy's story is a familiar one. But the happy ending is that *being* forgiven has nothing to do with *feeling* forgiven. Being forgiven has to do with what God did for us.

Lest we think that forgiving ourselves is a modern dilemma, consider Peter and Paul, who had to face the problem of forgiving themselves—in a very intense fashion.

After Peter refuted that he even knew Christ, "the Lord turned and looked at Peter. Then Peter remembered" (Luke 22:61 NKJV). How many times did Peter have to deal with that before he was able to forgive himself? He denied his Lord at a moment in His life when, if ever He needed a friend, it was then. This was the same Peter who said in effect, "Lord, all the rest of these may forsake You, but when everybody has forsaken You, You can count on the rock." Ironically, Peter was the very one He couldn't count on. Peter had to learn to forgive himself for that.

Then there was Paul before his conversion. His background, learning, and culture, his intensity and commitment to Jehovah God, and his faithfulness to Judaism all had been committed to removing Christianity—that growing, monstrous philosophy—from the face of this earth. He had been consumed with the task of eradicating from people's minds any remains of that person they called Jesus, and Paul had done everything he could to kill or destroy the Lord's church. Though our scriptural understanding of forgiveness is found most clearly in the writings of the apostle Paul, no doubt he too grappled with his own forgiveness.

Many of us are at—or have been at—that place in our lives. We struggle with forgiving ourselves for things we did in the past—some of those mistakes having occurred years and years ago.

. . . Perhaps adults who said cruel things as children or who engaged in sin as teenagers look back and vividly remember how they acted.

. . . Or some women who have had abortions experience a gnawing, haunting feeling of remorse deep down inside. Even though they've asked God and other people to forgive them, somehow they can't seem to forgive themselves.

. . . Or men and women who divorced their spouses realize they were wrong and cannot forgive themselves.

. . . Or parents who ran their children away from home, and their children's lives were wrecked and ruined as a result, can't forgive themselves for being the cause.

Yet *the ability or capacity to forgive ourselves is absolutely essential* if any peace whatsoever is to be found.

> He has not dealt with us according to our sins,
> Nor punished us according to our iniquities.
> For as the heavens are high above the earth,
> So great is His mercy toward those who fear Him;
> As far as the east is from the west,
> So far has He removed our transgressions from us.
> As a father pities his children,
> So the LORD pities those who fear Him.
> For He knows our frame;
> He remembers that we are dust. (Ps. 103:10–14 NKJV)

These verses inspired by the Holy Spirit are a beautiful assurance to us that God is a forgiving Father.

CONSEQUENCES OF NOT FORGIVING OURSELVES

The problem is that some of us are not able to forgive ourselves. We look at whatever we've done and think that we are beyond forgiveness. But what we really feel is disappointment in ourselves—a disappointment that confuses measurement of our sin with merit for our forgiveness.

Sin and self-forgiveness tend to assume inverse proportions in our minds—that is, the greater our sin, the lesser our forgiveness. Similarly, the lesser our sin, the greater our forgiveness. Would we, for instance, withhold forgiveness from ourselves for saying unpleasant things about a friend? pocketing the extra money when a clerk returns the wrong change? putting someone down and pretending it's all in good fun? lying about why we're late coming home? having an abortion? calling a child stupid or dumb? injuring or killing a person while driving intoxicated? fornicating or committing adultery?

We may not think we would be capable of some sins, but not a single one of us fully knows how we would act if we found ourselves in different circumstances. Although some sins bring greater condemnation or chastisement in the life of believers, God's viewpoint is that sin is sin. And just as God's viewpoint of sin covers all sins, so does His viewpoint of forgiveness. But when we choose not to forgive ourselves as God does, we can expect to experience the consequences of a self-directed unforgiving spirit.

Self-Punishment

The first consequence of a self-directed unforgiving spirit is that *we punish ourselves on an ongoing basis*. How do we do that? We replay our sins continually. Satan initiates it, and we foolishly follow. We even replay the feelings of guilt. And as we do, we put ourselves in a tortured state that God never intended.

If, for instance, we wake up in the morning under a load of guilt (*Oh, what have I done? I'm so ashamed. God can never forgive me. If my friends find out . . .*), we have put the burden on ourselves, not on God. We are unwilling to forgive ourselves, even though as believers and children of God we are already forgiven. We get up, work, play, go to bed, and sleep in a self-imposed bondage, in a prison we build ourselves.

We spiritually incarcerate ourselves despite the fact that *no* place in the Bible does God say He has forgiven us of all our sins "except . . ." Jesus paid it all. Jesus bore in His body the price for *all* our sins. No exceptions.

Uncertainty

The second consequence of a self-directed unforgiving spirit is that *we live under a cloud of uncertainty*. We do not accept our forgiveness by God; we exist under an abiding question mark. If we never forgive ourselves, we can never be confident that God has forgiven us—and we bear the weight of this guilt. We are not quite sure of where we stand with God. We are not quite sure what He may do next, because if we are not worthy of His blessing . . .

Sometimes this cloud of uncertainty is deep and dark. Sometimes it is not so dark, but because our understanding and our acceptance of God's forgiveness are limited by our own guesswork, we are not at all sure how God intends to handle us and our transgressions. And so we pass up the peace that passes all understanding, and we have no contentment.

If we refuse to forgive ourselves—despite the fact that God has *not* dealt with us according to our sins, that God has *not* rewarded us according to our iniquities—we continue to live under that cloud of uncertainty.

Sense of Unworthiness

The third consequence of a self-directed unforgiving spirit is that *we develop a sense of unworthiness*. Because we are guilty, we also feel unworthy.

But when we hold ourselves accountable for our sins, we are indulging in a guilt-trip. Satan encourages guilt-trips. He may inject these ideas in our thoughts: *Why should God answer my prayer? He is not going to hear what I am saying. Look what I have done.* Satan punches the button, and we replay the past sin. Satan keeps getting us to replay in our minds what God says He has forgotten—and we guiltily oblige. And each time we replay the past sin by not forgiving ourselves, our faith takes a beating and we feel unworthy. This sense of unworthiness affects our prayer life, our intimate relationship with God, and our service for Him.

To a great degree, we paralyze our usefulness before God when we allow our guilt to cause us to feebly—and always unsuccessfully—attempt payment for our sins when Jesus already paid the debt two thousand years ago for *all* our sins.

Excessive Behavior

The fourth consequence of a self-directed unforgiving spirit is that *we attempt to overcome our guilt by compulsive behavior and excesses in our lives*. We try drugs, alcohol, sexual affairs, material possessions.

Whenever we dedicate huge amounts of energy to divert our attention from the real problem (our unwillingness to forgive ourselves), we try to escape from the incessant self-pronouncements of guilt. Some of us invest huge amounts of energy into work—we work harder, faster, longer. But no matter how furiously we work, our guilt cannot be diminished by our frantic pace. Sometimes we take on two, three, or four jobs in the church to prove our dedication. We teach Sunday school, sing in the choir, and visit the shut-ins. What servants of God! And we end up making nervous wrecks of ourselves.

Compulsive behavior of this sort is akin to saying, "God, I want to thank You for Jesus' death on the cross, but it wasn't enough." So because we do not accept God's forgiveness, we double our efforts. (Do we really think that God wasn't able to do it alone? That He needs *our* help?) And we begin a self-feeding, spiritually defeating cycle.

The only real answer to our dilemma is to accept God's forgiveness and to forgive ourselves. We may think, *I can't forgive myself for what I have done.* But God gave us the rebuttal to that type of thinking. When Jesus took our sins upon Himself, it's as if He said, "I have come to liberate you. I have come to free you. I have come to set the captives free." If we do not forgive ourselves because of our unworthiness, we miss the point of Jesus' death on the cross.

False Humility

The fifth consequence of a self-directed unforgiving spirit is that *we develop a false sense of humility when we feel permanently judged guilty and sentenced by God.* We wear but a facade of humility when we declare ourselves so unworthy to serve God. And our "humble face" serves as a mask to keep us from seeing our true face.

Does this sound familiar? We may be complimented: "That was absolutely marvelous!" But then we respond, "I don't deserve your praise. Just give God all the praise and the glory." Sometimes that's a sincere response, but sometimes that's a response motivated by a guilty complex. When we harbor a false sense of humility, it's very difficult to accept a compliment.

Actually, none of us (I no more than you) are worthy of praise. We are worthy solely because of God's truth that "we are His workmanship, created in Christ Jesus for good works" (Eph. 2:10 NKJV). It is amazing how a self-directed unforgiving spirit distorts our viewpoint and perverts our thinking. It makes us harbor and nourish—even covet—our past errors so that we wallow in fake humility. We become focused on ourselves and on our unworthiness and on our humility.

Believers need look back only in thanksgiving to the grace of God. Believers can look to the now for what God is doing—and to the future for what God will continue to do.

Self-Deprivation

The sixth consequence of a self-directed unforgiving spirit is that *we deprive ourselves of things God wants us to enjoy.* Self-deprivation is the opposite of compulsive behavior and excesses. We say things like, "Oh, I couldn't buy myself that. I couldn't go there. I couldn't do that."

Self-deprivation is like an acid that eats away at the truth of Jesus' sacrifice. We do not achieve a state of forgiveness by arbitrarily abstaining from good things in our lives. God does not ask us to deprive ourselves in order to "deserve" forgiveness. Self-deprivation is self-choice, not God's choice. Do we presume to know something about our sin that God does not know? Do we dare think that we have some new information about sin and forgiveness that God does not have? Of course not. If our sovereign, holy, righteous God has seen fit in His omniscience to declare us not guilty and to forgive us our sin, we have no grounds for self-deprivation.

To deny ourselves forgiveness and to put ourselves through

unending punishment is to sentence ourselves to hell on earth. Satan is a master at deception, and it is Satan who makes us think that we have to suffer until God says, "Okay, that's enough." At what point do we think we will be free? When will we have suffered enough? It is apparent that this type of thinking is absurd, yet many believers act as if they think that's how God's forgiveness works.

An unforgiving spirit is actually *unbelief.* We fail to exercise faith in God if we fail to forgive ourselves *when Christ says He has paid the penalty.* Why would He pay the penalty if we have yet to pay it? Christ paid the penalty so that we would be pardoned, but that does not mean that our pardon eliminates every problem. The aftereffects of sin may linger, and even if we forgive ourselves, we still have to deal with the consequences of our sin.

Satan may try to hinder our understanding of forgiveness by insinuating selfish motives. *I know why you are trying to believe that. You are just trying to get off scot-free.* But we must not allow Satan to twist the truth in our thoughts. We need to repel his influence by remembering that, indeed, there was nothing "free" about the Cross. The ultimate price was exacted and paid.

Talking about grace isn't enough; we must *live* by grace. If we think we can be forgiven by doing anything other than accepting the blood of our Lord, our theology is warped.

WHY WE CAN'T FORGIVE OURSELVES

Since we know the negative consequences from not forgiving ourselves, what stands in our way? What hinders our acceptance of God's forgiveness on our own behalf? Our resistance generally can be traced to one of four general problem areas:

(1) belief in performance-based forgiveness; (2) disappointment in self; (3) adjustment and surrender to guilt; and (4) expectation of repeated sin.

Belief in Performance-Based Forgiveness

Performance-based forgiveness is not biblically based forgiveness. We can't "pay" for God's unlimited forgiveness by working harder or serving more fervently. The Bible says that God accepts us on the basis of what He did, not on the basis of what we try to do. But we tend to rationalize. *I have got to measure up.* Ever since we were children, we have learned that whatever we achieve or receive we do so as a result of our own actions.

"Mom, can I have a cookie?"

"If you are good."

Performance. Our whole lives are based on performance. *If I clean my room, Mom will let me do this. If I take out the trash, Dad will let me do that. If I do well at the tryouts, I may make the team.*

Then, when it comes to the grace of God and the Bible's teachings, what happens? No performance is required. *Hold it*, we may think. *That isn't right.* But it is right—God's idea of forgiveness is in a category all by itself.

As believers, we are forgiven children of God, no matter what we do. This does *not* mean, however, that we can do whatever we like and go merrily on our way. It means that as believers we have already been forgiven of our sins—past, present, and future—whether we confess them or not. We don't have to keep asking for forgiveness and keep working to pay for it.

Our difficulty is not one of being unforgiven; it is one of *feeling* unforgiven. We are separated from God by sin, not by lack of forgiveness. Believers are always forgiven. Grace is an unmerited, undeserved, nonnegotiable gift from God that comes to us prepaid. It can't be purchased, and it is offered freely to all who receive it. And that's what the grace of God is all about.

Disappointment in Self

We sometimes have a difficult time accepting the truth about ourselves. I can remember a personal experience where God had done a marvelous work in my life. The Lord was blessing me, and I was just moving right along. Then I acted in a very disappointing way. I knew better, but I blew it horribly. The Lord had lifted me up, and I fell flat on my face. I still remember the feelings of shame and depression.

I wrestled with God's forgiveness for a short period of time before I was able to accept it. At least I thought I accepted it. Because I had sorely disappointed myself, it was difficult for me to forgive myself for not living up to my own expectations.

It is important to realize that we disappoint ourselves; we don't disappoint God. How can we disappoint Someone who already knows what we're going to do? Disappointment is the result of unfulfilled expectations, and God doesn't expect anything of us. God knows that we are going to blow it. And that's what the grace of God is all about.

Adjustment and Surrender to Guilt

Emotionally, we may live so long under guilt and self-condemnation that the very idea of being free is threatening. We feel comfortable with what we know, and what we know is guilt. We adjust to our feelings of guilt and surrender the peace we could enjoy if we forgave ourselves.

I have counseled people and clearly outlined what the Bible has to say about their particular problem. After professing understanding, these same people may end up praying the same old prayer they pray all the time, and when they finish praying, they haven't dealt with the issue.

If we want to be released from guilt, we must change our thinking. We need a thorough cleansing of our thought processes. No more thinking, *I know what the Bible says about forgiveness, but*—Every time we include a *but*, we put one more bar in our prison of guilt. We need to get rid of the bars; we need to break out of the prison. We don't have to be there. But we have to want to get out.

Expectation of Repeated Sin

I know God could forgive me. And I know He has forgiven me. I guess the reason I don't forgive myself is that I know I am going to repeat that sin. These are the thoughts that cause us so much trouble.

How many sins did we commit before the Cross? We weren't even in existence two thousand years ago. All *our* sins for which Christ died were in the future, including sins that we commit over and over again. God's forgiveness is all-inclusive, regardless of the nature of our sins or the frequency of our indulgence.

This does *not* mean we escape the consequences of our sins simply because we are forgiven. This means that we are assured forever of forgiveness, that we need not withhold forgiveness from ourselves because we may sin again. God forgives us every time for every sin, and so must we.

HOW WE CAN FORGIVE OURSELVES

How do we forgive ourselves? Regardless of how long we have been in bondage, we can be free if we follow four biblical steps.

Step 1. Recognize the Problem

We must recognize and acknowledge that we have not forgiven ourselves. We must come to grips with the fact that we still hold ourselves in bondage. *Father, I realize I haven't forgiven myself and am in bondage because of it.*

Step 2. Repent of Sin

We must repent of that sin for which we cannot forgive ourselves. We must tell God that we realize that our unwillingness to forgive ourselves is not in keeping with His Word. And we must thank Him for His forgiveness as we confess our sin to Him. *I thank You, Father, for forgiving me for holding myself in bondage, for keeping myself from You, and for limiting Your use of me.*

Step 3. Reaffirm Trust

We must reaffirm our trust in the testimony of Scripture: "As far as the east is from the west, so far has He removed our transgressions from us" (Ps. 103:12 NKJV). *Father, I reaffirm my trust and my faith in the Word of God.*

Step 4. Confess Freedom and Choose to Receive It

We must confess our freedom and choose to receive it freely. *Lord Jesus, on the basis of Your Word, by an act of my will, in faith, I here and now forgive myself because You have already forgiven me and I accept my forgiveness. I choose from this moment to be freed of all which I have held against myself. Please confirm my freedom to me by the power and presence of Your Holy Spirit.*

If we are willing to follow these simple steps, not only will we be set free, but the healing process will be initiated.

When we choose by an act of the will to accept what God

has said is true, we accept God's acceptance of us. And we can tell Him that we have played back that accusing video-tape for the last time. When Satan tries to punch the button again, he will find that he has been short-circuited by Jesus. We are free.

Questions for Personal Growth

1. Name and discuss six consequences of a self-directed unforgiving spirit.

2. What four problem areas usually stand in the way of accepting God's forgiveness? Why isn't it necessary to measure up to God's forgiveness?

3. Name four biblical steps to forgiveness.

4. Do you understand the point of Jesus' death on the cross? Put in writing your understanding of Jesus' death on the cross as it relates to your sins—past, present, and future.

Ten

BITTERNESS

Bitterness often lies beneath our inability to forgive and be forgiven. It is a corrosive culprit that denies our peace and destroys our relationships.

The Bible cautions us about the root of bitterness:

> See to it that no one comes short of the grace of God; that no root of bitterness springing up causes trouble, and by it many be defiled. (Heb. 12:15)

The Greek word for bitterness (*pikria*) comes from the root word *pik*, which means "to cut," and therefore, "pointed" or "sharp." It refers to what is cutting and sharp. It also implies "bitter taste." Verse 15 refers metaphorically to bitter fruit produced by the root of bitterness.

As I have counseled hurting people over the past three decades, I have helped them discover bitter roots they had been nurturing for weeks, months, and often years. We can be bitter and hide it from the rest of the world by disguising it as various other attitudes. We express bitterness in our lives in a number of ways—anger, passion, slander, malice. But we cannot hide our bitterness from God, or even from our own bodies.

Bitterness is *never* constructive; bitterness is *always* destructive. It doesn't make any difference what people have done to us or how bad it was or how often they did it. Bitterness as a response to wrongdoing is never acceptable before God. Nothing good ever comes from bitterness.

"*See to it* . . ." That is, be diligent. The word *see*, as it is used in verse 15, is derived from the same combination of Greek roots—*epi* ("upon") and *skopeo* ("to look at," "contemplate")—that gives us the word *oversight*. As Christians, we are charged with a duty to fulfill.

"*That no one comes short of the grace of God* . . ." We are to care for one another and see to it that we live in grace. We are to respond *in* grace *to* grace. We can't allow ourselves to slip over into our old lifestyles. As Christians, we can no longer respond to hurts, abuse, cheating, criticism, lies, and rejection in any way other than how our Lord responds to us—with forgiveness.

"*That no root of bitterness springing up* . . ." The day we received Jesus as our Savior, we forsook all rights to be bitter. We must put all bitterness from us and guard against its taking root in our lives—no matter what happens, no matter how despicably we are treated.

We tend to think, however, that individual, personal circumstances are clearly exceptions. A deliberate smear campaign against us, for instance. Or a husband who walks out on his forty-three-year-old wife and takes up with a twenty-one-year-old. Or a wife who betrays her husband for the fleeting sensation of a weekend affair. Or children who reject their parents' values and play the life of idle degenerates after having been brought up in godly homes. Or women who are held back because they're the wrong sex, or men who are passed over for promotion because they're the wrong color. Or employees who are fired to make room for the boss's friends and family members. Or retirees who are struck with severe disability after having waited years to enjoy the fruits of their labor.

Bitterness can be "justified" so easily. *Well, I have a right to be bitter. He knew I was after that account, and just when I was about to close the deal, he lied about my qualifications. That cost me a bundle, and I'm sure not going to smile and say it's okay. He hurt me, and he's not going to get away with it.* But we must be careful not to allow bitterness to take root in our lives. As a root has fine tentacles that reach out for moisture in order to grow, just so does a root of bitterness have tentacles that reach out. The root of bitterness needs feedback, little evidences of its right for existence, in order to grow. It is fed by our misconceived notions that we have a "right" to feel bitter. But the truth is that believers have no right to respond with bitterness.

I recently read a best-seller, the autobiography of a successful businessman. In the beginning of the book, the author related a tragic event, and in telling the story, he said he would never forgive the person who had wronged him. As I continued to read, however, a cloud hung over all the exciting things that this man accomplished. *For that I will never forgive him.* What that person did was so bad that the author intended to be that person's emotional slave for the rest of his life! Regardless of wealth, fame, or popularity, if we allow bitterness to take root, we relinquish control of our lives. We cannot live with bitterness, because bitterness will eat away at us until we are destroyed.

THE EFFECTS OF BITTERNESS

"*Causes trouble, and by it many be defiled.*" We may not even be consciously aware that we are nursing bitter feelings, but the effects of bitterness are subtle and many.

Physical Illnesses

A friend of mine is a fine man and a fine pastor who loves God. His wife had cancer, and they sought the best medical help. I'll call them the Browns. The doctor, who had been studying the relationship between cancer and negative emotions, began to work with Mrs. Brown. He went to see her every day, and every day he would try to get her to talk about her past. Week after week, he tried his best to get her to cry. She wouldn't cry. She couldn't cry. Somehow, there simply was nothing to cry about.

But the doctor and Mrs. Brown kept on talking. And one day, in the midst of their conversation, she began to cry. As the tears gushed out, she confessed bitterness toward her parents for something that had happened years ago. When she got it all out, she was freed, liberated, and forgiven. Today Mrs. Brown stands by her husband's side with love and support for his ministry. It is the doctor's opinion that she would not have recovered had she not rid herself of bitterness.

Though we can't see what is happening on the inside, often we see visible, outer results. Bitterness is like a continually running machine that uses our bodies for its energy source. It runs when we are sleeping, it runs when we are talking with our friends, and it runs when we are simply sitting and being quiet. Because bitterness is a lifestyle and not an isolated occurrence, it never shuts down. It keeps operating and draining energy.

It is impossible to be bitter very long without affecting our bodies. More and more, medical professionals are beginning to see some kind of link between the way our bodies function and the way we think. Bitterness, anger, and other negative emotions have been associated with glandular problems, high blood pressure, cardiac disorders, ulcers, and a host of other physical ailments.

Stained Relationships

Bitterness causes one person trouble and defiles others. As used in Hebrews 12:15, the Greek word for defile *(miaino)* means "to stain" or "to dye." The bitterness we nourish will stain our relationships. This is one reason why there are so many separations, divorces, and broken homes.

A young couple—John and Linda—got married. Unbeknownst to either, John came into the marriage with a root of bitterness. Linda tried to love him, but in spite of all her attempts, she couldn't get through to him. She just could not tunnel through John's hardened emotional wall. It had been there for years—ever since he was twelve and his mother had died. Throughout his growing years, John had camouflaged his bitterness. He had been successful in keeping it well hidden until after his marriage. Then when Linda settled into marriage and began to be herself, all of a sudden she was facing a marriage partner whom she loved dearly but could not communicate with. John couldn't let down his defenses. He couldn't be himself.

Linda and John tried to discover their problem. Why did he feel the way he did? Why couldn't he return Linda's love? Even John didn't know why he was unable to love. *Where did it all start? Why can't I love? Why do I have these feelings? Why can't I be myself? Why can't I relax? Why do I have this stress?*

Why am I critical? Why am I negative about things? What is going on in my life? John wasn't able to raise the mental blinds and discover the source of his problem—bitterness. He was angry with his mother, and his bitterness toward her was staining his marriage.

Much of the time the cause of such problems is found to be an unforgiving spirit that has taken bitter root. As in John and Linda's case, John couldn't forgive his mother for dying and leaving him.

Bitterness can paralyze us. Even when we genuinely want to love another person, we can't. It is not that we don't want to—we simply can't. Parents wonder why they can't love their children. Children wonder why they can't love their parents. Husbands and wives wonder why they can't love their spouses, why they can't break through the barrier. But deep inside, they may find themselves infected by roots of bitterness and resentment, even simmering hatred.

Let me relate another example. Ed and Nancy had a storybook wedding, and they excitedly made plans for their family. They would have a boy and a girl, just as Nancy had dreamed for years. When Nancy got pregnant, they were overjoyed, and when she delivered a firstborn boy, they were ecstatic. About a year and a half later, she got pregnant again. But this time there were complications, and the doctor told them this would be their last child. No matter. They had their boy, Michael, and now they would have their girl. Their family would be complete. Except they didn't have a daughter, they had another boy—Jason.

At first Nancy was despondent, but she soon got over her disappointment—she thought. Michael and Jason were both little charmers. As the two boys grew, however, little differences began to emerge. Michael could do no wrong, it seemed, but

Jason was forever getting in trouble. Nancy found herself picking at Jason and criticizing him no matter what he did. Ed traveled a great deal in his sales job, and so for a while he didn't notice anything unusual in Nancy's treatment of the boys. When she yelled at Jason, Ed thought she was just tired from running after the boys all day. But when the boys were ages six and four, Ed spent his vacation at home instead of taking the family on their usual vacation rounds. As he puttered around the house, it became evident to him that Nancy adored Michael but could hardly stand Jason. Ed suggested counseling, and Nancy agreed.

During counseling, Nancy confessed that she hated Jason because he had robbed her of the little girl she had always wanted. She could not forgive Jason. Moreover, Nancy felt that Ed couldn't love her if he refused to understand that Jason had ruined her life. Nancy clung to her unforgiving spirit, and the root of bitterness assumed control over her life. She divorced Ed, and he gained custody of the two boys—she didn't even want her beloved Michael around her at that point, because in her mind, she thought he too would someday turn against her. Nancy felt she had plenty of reasons to be bitter. In actuality, her unforgiving spirit fed her bitterness, and the root of bitterness had grown so huge it tainted the lives of her husband and sons.

Bitterness has so many little sprouts to it. Distrust is one of them. Insecurity is another. When the Bible says "see to it that . . . no root of bitterness (springs) up," it is because the consequences are awesome and ongoing.

Spiritual Stumbling Blocks

Bitterness creates a cloak of guilt. We know we shouldn't feel the way we do toward others, and we know God doesn't want us to be full of resentment. And, our reasoning goes, if God isn't pleased with us, how can He accept us? We sense a barrier between God and ourselves and begin to doubt our salvation. How in the world are we going to be secure in our salvation when this turmoil, this civil war, is constantly going on?

Bitterness also hinders our influence for Christ. What kind of Christian testimony can we have if we are bitter toward God and toward our neighbors? How can we convincingly talk to others about the forgiveness of God when we refuse to forgive those who have wronged us? When we allow bitterness to take over our lives, that bitterness spills over into the lives of those around us.

As I noted earlier, not long ago I sat down with my two children, Andy and Becky, and asked if they had resentful feelings toward me for any wrong I had perpetrated. At the time, they were both in their twenties, and so they felt freer to talk openly and honestly.

Andy was the first to respond. He recalled the time when he was thirteen or fourteen and was practicing one part of a song. Over and over, the same melody. I asked him if that was all he knew. Andy recalled that to his adolescent ears, my words sounded as if I were saying, "I don't like you or your music." That damaging impression caused him to decide not to play any music for me again, even though he was a talented musician.

Becky had her memory too. "When I was five years old, we lived in Miami. One day you put me in my room and you wouldn't let me out. I cried and cried, but you wouldn't let me out."

I asked their forgiveness on both matters, as well as on a few others. What I had quickly said and done and just as quickly forgotten, Andy and Becky had not forgotten. I had gone on for years without knowing that I had hurt them.

How many of us harbor those little things that caused us to feel rejected? How many of us today are angry adults because we don't feel loved? As we think of those who have hurt us or wronged us, we need to deal with those feelings. Some things may have been said or done long ago, so long ago that we don't think we feel their sting anymore, but our thoughts are affected. An unforgiving spirit is a devastating emotion that none of us can afford.

The devastation of bitterness is vividly depicted in the life of King Saul, who began his reign as a respected and favored ruler but who ended his life in defeat, sorrow, and suicide. The ravages of a bitter spirit toward David and toward God were instrumental in his demise.

In 1 Samuel 18:1–7 (NIV), Saul's seed of bitterness toward David is planted. David had come back from slaying Goliath, and the women played tambourines and lutes. They danced and sang, "Saul has slain his thousands, and David his tens of thousands" (v. 7). Their song did not set well with Saul. He "was very angry; this refrain galled him" (v. 8). David's fame enraged Saul. "And from that time on Saul kept a jealous eye on David" (v. 9). This is the way bitterness works. We become angry because of some incident. David had saved Saul's reputation in fighting Goliath and defeating him for the cause of Jehovah God. But instead of being indebted to David, Saul became angry, suspicious, and then afraid.

The next day an evil spirit from God came forcefully upon Saul. He was prophesying in his house, while David was playing the harp, as he usually did. Saul had a spear in his hand and he hurled it, saying to himself, "I'll pin David to the wall." But David eluded him twice.

Saul was afraid of David, because the LORD was with David but had left Saul. (1 Sam. 18:10–12 NIV)

Saul was afraid of David's competition for the kingdom, even though David had made no move toward that end. "So he sent David away from him and gave him command over a thousand men, and David led the troops in their campaigns" (v. 13). And so Saul separated himself from David. Bitterness drives a hard wedge between even the best of friends.

Saul said to David, "Here is my older daughter Merab. I will give her to you in marriage; only serve me bravely and fight the battles of the LORD." For Saul said to himself, "I will not raise a hand against him. Let the Philistines do that!" (1 Sam. 18:17 NIV)

Bitterness eventually develops into scheming and plotting. We, like Saul, begin to manipulate events that are harmful to the other party. We arrive at the point where we would like to inflict all the vengeance possible on that person. If we can't, then maybe somebody else can. We just stand back and smile. I have heard of men and women who have divorced their spouses years ago and yet are still scheming to get their vengeance. They are still hoping that circumstances will destroy the former spouses in some form or fashion.

I went fishing one time with a man who had a responsible position in his corporation, but he wanted to be president. He informed me he was going to get that position, even if he had to stomp all over the current president. He did it too. He destroyed the other man, and he became president. But within eighteen months, he had destroyed himself as well.

When bitterness becomes our master, we act foolishly and

irrationally. Saul even tried to cast his javelin straight through his own son's heart when Jonathan questioned Saul's vengeance toward David.

> Saul's anger flared up at Jonathan and he said to him, "You son of a perverse and rebellious woman! Don't I know that you have sided with the son of Jesse to your own shame and to the shame of the mother who bore you? As long as the son of Jesse lives on this earth, neither you nor your kingdom will be established. Now send and bring him to me, for he must die!"
>
> "Why should he be put to death? What has he done?" Jonathan asked his father. But Saul hurled his spear at him to kill him. Then Jonathan knew that his father intended to kill David. (1 Sam. 20:30–33 NIV)

Bitter, angry parents often fling verbal javelins at their children, shattering their children's self-esteem, their sense of belonging, their sense of competency. Parents, impelled by bitter attitudes, can destroy their children with bitter attitudes, just as Saul, in a terrible fit of anger, tried to kill his own son. Saul argued that his deadly vengeance against David was to protect the kingdom for Jonathan, but Jonathan's probing question— "What has he done?"—was more than Saul could handle.

Saul was destroyed by bitterness. What had begun as anger developed into suspicion, fear, separation, insecurity, and vengeance. Saul's bitterness took control over his life. He seethed with hatred toward David and sought to plot his murder. He behaved irrationally toward his son, Jonathan. Saul's bitterness spilled over into the lives of many innocent people and caused a whole town of priests to be destroyed. Because of his bitterness, Saul could no longer hear from God.

I believe Saul's bitterness began *before* David killed Goliath and the townswomen taunted him with song. Saul's bitterness began when Samuel told him that he had lost the kingdom: "The LORD has torn the kingdom of Israel from you today and has given it to one of your neighbors—to one better than you" (1 Sam. 15:28 NIV). Saul was bitter toward God, but since it's a little tough to say so, Saul directed his bitterness toward David.

Saul paid an awful price for his bitterness toward a man God favored. Every action Saul took against David was turned to David's advantage. David became Israel's greatest king and most beloved writer in the Old Testament. We can learn from David's example. If we are targets of someone's bitterness, we can believe that God will do for us according to His will for our lives. What He did for David, He will do for us if we respond in His will.

RECOVERY FROM BITTERNESS

How can we recover from the effects of bitterness? *Recover* means "to get back" or "to regain." To recover from an illness, for example, means to get back or regain one's health. To recover from bitterness, then, means to get back or regain one's sweet or even temper.

When the root of bitterness has been growing a long time, its removal is not always instantaneous. A husband and wife who decide to get back together after having been separated can honestly confess to each other and repent of their sins, but full restoration comes gradually. The inner healing of the spirit sometimes takes longer than the physical healing of a broken arm or leg, for instance. We may have lived with damaged emotions for years, perhaps since childhood. As children of God, however, we have the capacity to forgive and to root out bitterness from our lives, even when it causes us temporary loss or humiliation. Unless we forgive, we cannot love.

Getting Motivated to Deal with Bitterness

How can we be motivated to forgive and to root out bitterness? We need to heed the call of our Lord Jesus Christ to forgive others. In the Sermon on the Mount, Jesus said:

> Be merciful, just as your Father also is merciful. Judge not, and you shall not be judged. Condemn not, and you shall not be condemned. Forgive, and you will be forgiven. (Luke 6:36–37 NKJV)

Jesus did not mean that our heavenly Father will not forgive us if we haven't forgiven others. Jesus meant that if we don't emotionally release those who have wronged us, God will keep the pressure on us until we do, because He wants us to be reconciled.

When we fully comprehend God's forgiveness toward us, we simply cannot justify our holding anyone else accountable. Throughout Jesus' ministry, He consistently taught forgiveness. But not only did He proclaim it, He demonstrated it with His words from the cross: "Father, forgive them; for they do not know what they are doing" (Luke 23:34).

Because Christ dwells in us as believers, we have a spiritual nature to forgive. We received this new spiritual nature when we received Christ. Paul put it this way:

> I have been crucified with Christ and I no longer live, but Christ lives in me. The life I live in the body, I live by faith in the Son of God, who loved me and gave himself for me. (Gal. 2:20 NIV)

The life we live is an expression of the life of Christ. We have the capacity to forgive when we have been deeply hurt because Christ within us is able to release through us forgiveness toward anyone. Just as Jesus forgave those who crucified Him, His life within us makes it possible for us to forgive all kinds of hurt and abuse, even in the most heinous forms. Because we are children of God, it is out of character for us to have unforgiving spirits and allow bitter roots to take hold.

Jesus never withheld forgiveness; so too we should never withhold forgiveness. By faith we can allow Christ to express that forgiveness through us toward others.

As we forgive one another, we release ourselves from bitterness. Emotional release enables physical and spiritual healing, and it frees us from bondage to other people. As we forgive one another, we enjoy reconciliation and the joy of healthy, loving relationships.

Getting Rid of Bitterness

Getting rid of bitterness is a step-by-step process that leads toward emotional liberation and spiritual freedom. The steps are simple. As you are reading this, the face of someone toward whom you feel bitter has probably come to mind. Keep that person (or persons) in mind as you continue.

1. Make a list of the ways in which that person has offended you.

2. Make a list of your own faults.

3. Make a list of things you have done and for which God has forgiven you.

4. Ask God to help you view that person who has wronged you as a tool in the hand of God.

5. Ask God to forgive you for your bitterness toward that person.

6. Decide in your heart to assume total responsibility for your attitude.

7. If you feel it is appropriate, and will not cause more problems than it solves, go to that person, confess your bitterness, and ask for forgiveness. Remember, you are assuming the responsibility for your attitude; you are not trying to solicit repentance.

8. We have but two choices: We can allow bitterness to destroy us, or we can allow God to develop us into the persons He wants us to be. We must *choose* to view our circumstances and hurts as tools to be used by God to further develop our spiritual lives.

QUESTIONS FOR PERSONAL GROWTH

1. Explain how bitterness can take control over your life and put you in bondage.

2. Give some examples of how bitterness can affect people physically. Have you ever made yourself sick because of bitterness?

3. How does bitterness taint relationships? Has your bitterness ever spilled over into other people's lives? Explain.

4. Are you harboring slights or hurts that made you feel rejected, even though they may have occurred long ago? Name the seven steps you can take to get rid of bitterness. With one person in mind, then another, begin taking those steps.

Eleven

WHEN A BROTHER STUMBLES

I remember as a young boy being required to take a battery of fitness tests at the school gym. There were ropes tied to the ceiling I had to climb, mats rolled out for tumbling exercises, parallel bars I had to walk with my hands, and the like.

I distinctly recall the balance-beam drill. Remember that one? There was a long, skinny board about a half-inch thick we had to traverse backward and forward. We usually all sat around laughing and waiting for the inevitable slip to happen. Occasionally, some fellows would survive without a bobble, but even they eventually succumbed when boyish pride brought them back for a repeat attempt.

Sometimes I think we set up similar spiritual gymnastics for believers. Once saved, we Christians often unwittingly watch to see if our brothers can walk the straight and narrow way with nary a stumble or miscalculation.

It's an outlandish expectation, of course, since our pilgrimage on earth stretches over decades, and it is fraught at each daily turn with alluring, disorienting distractions and temptations, all capable of throwing us mildly or wildly off balance in our walk with the Savior.

Thus, when a brother stumbles on what Isaiah termed the "Highway of Holiness" (35:8), we should not be overly shocked. But we are. We shake our heads and wonder, *How could such a fine brother in Christ do such a shameful thing?*

Our reaction at this point is pivotal. Will we degenerate into useless gossip, pontificate with self-righteous judgment, stand silently by and see if the victim can somehow extricate himself from his fallen state, or will we extend the redemptive, rescuing arm of forgiveness?

Understanding why a believer falls into sin and grasping God's principles for helping him regain his upright walk will prepare us to be God's agents of reconciliation when a brother in Christ stumbles into transgression. (After all, at some point in time, each of us will be that brother.)

WE ALL SIN

All believers are subject to stumbling. The Word of God gives three very distinct reasons why we are prone to do this.

Sin Within Us

First, the Scriptures reveal that the principle of sin is still within us. No matter how committed we are to Christ or how well we understand the dynamics of the Holy Spirit, an active sin principle crouches within our hearts. Paul describes the turmoil it can generate:

For the good that I wish, I do not do; but I practice the very evil that I do not wish. But if I am doing the very thing I do not wish, I am no longer the one doing it, but sin which dwells in me. I find then the principle that evil is present in me, the one who wishes to do good. (Rom. 7:19–21)

Paul is not implying that sin is stronger than the power of the indwelling Spirit; he is making the point that it still exists and exerts a strong downward pull. Believers can resist and overcome the power of sin through the overcoming life of Christ, but there is a battle to be fought. For various reasons, we don't always share in the triumph that is ours through Calvary.

A Formidable Foe

Second, we stumble because we have an enemy who seeks to devour, deter, and detour us. He is called by many names— the Prince of this Age, the Prince of the Power of the Air, the Adversary, the Accuser of the Brethren—namely, Satan.

He is always there to harass us, tempt us, put pressure on us, and cause us to fail. He is the Accuser of the Brethren, not of unbelievers. Since he has failed in blinding our eyes to the truth of salvation, he will try to do the next best thing, which is to render us ineffective, frustrated, discouraged, and defeated for fruitful living and service. Luring us into repeated sin and launching ongoing forays into our more vulnerable areas of personality or character are major tactics that work far too often and too effectively.

An Evil World System

Third, we live in an evil world system, thoroughly permeated by the vile spirit of the evil one. Books, arts, government, education, business, and recreation are all part and parcel of what Paul referred to as "this present evil age" (Gal. 1:4). This *kosmos*, or fallen worldly system, is masterminded by

Satan himself and confronts believers on every front of daily living. We cannot escape it. Though we are not *of* the world, we are certainly *in it.*

This myriad of opposition is imposing enough to deal us toppling blows. Anyone who says, "I would never do this or that," is in reality setting the stage for an unflattering fall. This self-conferred standard of righteousness has lowered resistance in that particular area because the individual now rests on personal adequacy as a line of defense against a far superior foe. It's like guarding a fort with a water pistol.

WHY WE STUMBLE

The apostle Paul writes the biblical prescription for forgiving a fallen brother,

> Brethren, even if a man is caught in any trespass, you who are spiritual, restore such a one in a spirit of gentleness; each one looking to yourself, lest you too be tempted. Bear one another's burdens, and thus fulfill the law of Christ. For if anyone thinks he is something when he is nothing, he deceives himself. But let each one examine his own work, and then he will have reason for boasting in regard to himself alone, and not in regard to another. For each one shall bear his own load. (Gal. 6:1–5)

Notice Paul's use of the phrase "caught in any trespass." The idea expressed in the original language is one of a surprise, blunder, or fault. In other words, when Christians sin, we do not go out deliberately seeking to transgress. In a moment of weakness or indifference, we yield to or are ensnared by evil. We didn't start the morning by planning to lie, cheat, or lust, but as we walked in harm's way, we were wounded.

Knowing the Bible and God's ways as well as His warnings against sin, why do we still take bites out of the forbidden fruit?

Careless Living

The first factor that comes to mind is that we become careless in the Christian life. We fail to take the Bible's admonition about living "sensibly, righteously and godly in the present age" (Titus 2:12) as seriously as we should. We become careless in living out the truths we know and forget to take the kinds of precautions we ordinarily should to avoid Satan's snares.

Paul urges us, "Therefore be careful how you walk, not as unwise men, but as wise, making the most of your time, because the days are evil" (Eph. 5:15–16). People who are careless in their work are apt to have accidents that could have been avoided. Christians who develop sloppy prayer and study habits and who do not cultivate disciplined character traits under the tutelage of the Holy Spirit are prime targets for a fiery shaft of the enemy.

Ignorance

A second reason is ignorance. Sometimes we are unaware of sin and how Satan operates. Sometimes we are ignorant of ourselves and how we respond to certain temptations. Many times in the Scriptures, the writers declare: "Be not ignorant." One of the keys to Paul's overcoming life in the midst of such adversity was that he was not ignorant of Satan's schemes (2 Cor. 2:11). Neither should we be.

That is why we are continually challenged by God's Word to "press on toward the goal" (Phil. 3:14). We cannot be satisfied with what we already know. We need to learn so much truth to keep ourselves free from the yoke of sin that ever seeks to keep us in bondage.

Deception

A third reason believers stumble is deception. Satan lures us as an angel of light. He is crafty, cunning, and stealthy. He can cleverly camouflage his murderous traps with appealing enticements. If he could trick Adam and Eve, who enjoyed perfect, wonderful communion with Creator God, why do we think we can outwit him?

Pride

A fourth common denominator in tripping us up is pride. When we rely on our self-sufficiency or our self-effort to combat sin, rest assured that our waterloo is approaching. The "Big I" is no match for the Prince of Darkness. It's like an inflated balloon, just waiting to be deflated.

The Old Testament King Uzziah was a famous king and inventor. He was also a ferocious warrior who enjoyed great success "as long as he sought the LORD" (2 Chron. 26:5). He could have enjoyed a lifetime of victory if he hadn't enthroned the "Big I."

> Hence his fame spread afar, for he was marvelously helped until he was strong. But when he became strong, his heart was so proud that he acted corruptly, and he was unfaithful to the LORD his God, for he entered the temple of the LORD to burn incense on the altar of incense. (2 Chron. 26:15–16)

Uzziah was struck with leprosy by God for usurping the priests' functions, and his end was tragic. Pride will take us into places we have no business being, and it will not be long before we find ourselves overmatched.

Weariness

A fifth agent in causing believers to sin is weariness. We become physically or emotionally drained and are simply too weak to hold up the shield of faith. Our hands drop to our sides, the shield lies on the ground, and we become stationary targets for the incoming missiles. Elijah was ripe for fear and discouragement when Jezebel threatened him. This was probably because he had just finished running a marathon, beating King Ahab's chariot to Jezreel (1 Kings 18:45–46). His fatigue diluted his resistance.

Satanic Attack

A sixth factor is satanic attack. A satanic attack is a moment or a period of time of intense harassment from Satan, whereby individuals undergo absolutely arduous conflict with the powers of evil. They don't come only when we are close to sin. We can be praying, we can be working, we can be doing almost anything, and Satan can launch a major offensive against us.

Job encountered the blitzkrieg of Satan, losing his family and his possessions in a matter of hours. Though allowed by God, it nevertheless struck like a horde of locusts. That same intensity of persecution, still restrained and limited by almighty God, can swoop down on believers, especially if we are positioned in a place of fruitful service in the kingdom.

Pressure

A seventh reason is pressure. We buckle under the stress of job, family, and society and look for an emotional release valve that we feel will help meet a particular need at the moment. The strains and burdens become too much, and we struggle to open an escape hatch, not really caring where it may lead so long as it steers us out from under the load.

I think all of us who are honest with one another will have to admit, "Yes, I have failed." We haven't violated just one of the commandments. The truth is, we probably have violated all of them in some fashion or to some degree.

When we look back in the Old Testament, it is interesting to see that God's first three kings were all great men. Saul began his rule as an anointed leader. David was a noble ruler as well as an accomplished musician and poet. Solomon's wisdom has not been equaled.

Despite their success, however, they all stumbled. Saul's kingdom was stripped away because of his pride. David caved in to lust, and Solomon's sagacity was tragically marred by idolatry.

Christians today, no matter how strong, wise, or respected, are subject to some public or private manifestation of the sin principle. Believers who sow to the flesh will reap the same corrupt harvest as nonbelievers do. The flesh lusts against the Spirit and the Spirit against the flesh.

RESTORATION

Once the believer has blundered into transgression, the body of Christ has a God-given responsibility to restore the offenders: "Brethren, even if a man is caught in any trespass, you who are spiritual, restore such a one in a spirit of gentleness" (Gal. 6:1). The Scripture states a command, not a suggestion. It does not say we are to forgive someone who sins after we have examined the situation to discover guilt or innocence or if the person has suffered long enough for the indiscretion. It says we are to be involved in the restoration process, regardless of the nature of the sin.

The Greek word translated "restore" has medical overtones. The word picture is one of a physician who resets the bones of a broken limb. It portrays the setting straight of what was once crooked.

We can readily see the spiritual adaptation of this idea. Forgiving someone who falls is God's method of extending His healing for the wounded soul, helping put back together the joy and intimacy of blessed fellowship with the Father. We are to be the earthly vehicles by which the transgressor's brokenness is mended.

Jesus said, "For God did not send the Son into the world to judge [condemn] the world, but that the world should be saved through Him" (John 3:17). If the righteous Son of God was not to judge, we certainly do not have the right to judge someone caught by the web of sin. We may be discerning and wise, learning all we can for our own protection in such a situation, but we are never justified in condemning a fallen brother.

In fact, it is the specific task of the one who is "spiritual" to initiate the restoration of the one "caught in any trespass." This does not imply someone who has a haughty, superior attitude. It refers to someone who is daily walking under the leadership and influence of the Holy Spirit, someone who has accepted Christ as Savior and longs to see His lordship extended over every area of life.

Such individuals should exhibit the beautiful fruit of the Spirit. We should be caring, loving, forgiving, patient, and compassionate, not judgmental or holier-than-thou. Our actions should always be toward the healing and the recovery of the grieved brother.

Herein, though, is where many of us falter. We do not want to be associated with the sin the brother has been entangled in. We want to keep our distance. But we cannot mend bones from afar, and we cannot restore a shattered life from a prayer closet. If we are acquainted with the one who has sinned, however flagrantly or subtly, and we have a genuine, abiding relationship with the Savior, living as best we can under the dictates of the Spirit, we have a mandate from on high to be a part of helping administer the forgiveness of God.

Often we plead ignorance: "I just don't know how to help restore my friend. I'm afraid if I get involved, I may botch it up and make matters worse." Such sentiment is understandable, but it certainly is not biblical. We have the Holy Spirit. We have the Word of God. We have the love of the Spirit. We have the mind of Christ.

Do we want to see our bruised companion made whole again? If we do, we must ask God how He is going to use us as part of the spiritual rehabilitation. God will forgive the offense, but He may choose us to help bring that pardon through the following process.

SIX PRINCIPLES FOR RESTORATION

I believe if we implement the six principles listed below we will be scripturally equipped to assist in the restoration of a brother who has been ambushed or captured by sin.

Our first priority is to help the person *recognize the failure and the consequences* of the decision. The problem is not one of a slight miscue or a momentary lapse; it is a sin in the sight of the Lord. No one can deal with sin unless it is first identified as such. More often than not, the individual knows he has sinned, but he still lives in the tentacles of sin because he has not admitted that his behavior was sinful. Like David, the person must be able to confess, "I have sinned, and done what is evil in Thy sight" (Ps. 51:4).

We must help the person *acknowledge responsibility* for the sin. It is easy to blame sin on somebody else. But even if someone else has been a contributing factor, the individual is still accountable. Helping a brother assume personal culpability for sinful actions is sometimes a difficult but necessary step. Saul's life was characterized by obvious irresponsibility for his actions. He was always trying to blame someone else. When Samuel confronted Saul over his failure to utterly destroy the Amalekites, Saul responded, "But the people took some of the spoil, sheep and oxen" (1 Sam. 15:21).

We need to lead the person to *confess and repent* of the sin. By repentance, I mean a change of mind that will result in a true sense of regret and remorse over the sin as well as a deliberate change of behavior. The inner person will realize the grief of disobedience before God and eternal conduct will be positively affected.

The one who confesses and forsakes sin is the one who will prosper. This is a crucial step in redeeming the person for holy, fruitful living. Forgiveness is abundantly available through the blood of Calvary, but until true repentance occurs, the individual's heart is not ready to receive its cleansing power.

The fourth principle is one of *restitution*. Someone who steals something needs to pay it back. Someone who criticizes others in public needs to go to them and ask for forgiveness. Restitution cannot be made for some sins, however. Genuine repentance and confession will have to suffice in those instances. For example, there is no restitution for destroying a person's moral purity. Asking for forgiveness can restore Christlike fellowship, but it can never fully restore what was lost.

A fifth concern in reaching out with forgiveness to the

fallen brother is helping him receive *God's message* through his failure. Although God does not cause us to fail, He can teach us lessons that will keep us from wandering into similar harmful situations. His reproofs from such errors are invaluable: "He is on the path of life who heeds instruction, but he who forsakes reproof goes astray" (Prov. 10:17).

Finally, we need to guide the person who has fallen to *respond to God's chastisement with gratitude*. Granted, this is not easy, but when the person comprehends God's purpose in such discipline—that he might "share His holiness" (Heb. 12:10)—he can by an act of his will thank the heavenly Father for His loving correction. David said, "It is good for me that I was afflicted, that I may learn Thy statutes. The law of Thy mouth is better to me than thousands of gold and silver pieces" (Ps. 119:71–72). David saw the benefits of God's dealing with him and responded gratefully. Bringing the person to this point protects against the insidious root of bitterness that can spring up in the aftermath of sin.

THE SPIRIT OF RESTORATION

Our success in attempting to restore a fallen brother or sister will be determined to a great degree by the spirit in which we go about it. And what is the spirit in which we are to restore a fellow Christian? The answer to that question is found in our text:

> Brethren, even if a man is caught in any trespass, you who are spiritual, restore [let God use you to put back in place, to bring back, to reconcile] such a one in a spirit of gentleness; each one looking to yourself, lest you too be tempted. (Gal. 6:1)

First of all, Paul says we are to approach the guilty one in the *spirit of gentleness*. More than likely, the person is already hurting and as fragile as thin glass. Human chastisement, judgment, and condemnation would only worsen the individual's plight. Understanding and acceptance—not agreement, but acceptance—are needed instead.

This does not mean we are ignoring the place of chastisement in the process of restoration. But it is God's responsibility, not ours, to chastise. We are to restore a brother or sister in the spirit of gentleness, not in anger or in a passionate desire to defend the faith.

The spirit of gentleness means we are sensitive to the needs and to the hurt of the fallen one. Often the hurt, the regret, and the personal disappointment are overwhelming.

Second, we are to forgive and restore with the *spirit of humility*, recognizing that what happened to the other person could also happen to us. As fellow believers, we must help the individual recognize the sin, assume responsibility for sinful actions, repent of the sin, make restitution when possible, receive gladly the message God is sending through the failure, and thank Him for His loving chastisement. But if we do it with harshness and arrogance, we will only further damage, rather than restore, the brother or sister. We must be careful about our own lives, examining ourselves, knowing that we too are vulnerable to all types of temptation and sin.

When Paul writes to the Galatians, "Bear one another's burdens, and thus fulfill the law of Christ" (6:2), he adds a third dimension to the restoration process—the *spirit of love*. Jesus said, "By this all men will know that you are My disciples, if you have love for one another" (John 13:35). Again He said, "This is My commandment, that you love one another, just as I have loved you" (John 15:12). In the Galatians passage, the

word *burden* means a "heavy load." To bear someone's burden means we are willing to get under the load with him. We
are willing to share the weight of her hurt as she walks through
the valley of suffering or shame. We are willing to vicariously
suffer what he is suffering, to some degree feel what she is feeling. And we are to do this with love.

Jesus' encounter with the woman caught in adultery reveals
the folly of a condemning, rather than a loving, spirit.

> But Jesus went to the Mount of Olives. And early in the morn-
> ing He came again into the temple, and all the people were
> coming to Him; and He sat down ad began to teach them.
> And the scribes and the Pharisees brought a woman caught in
> adultery, and having set her in the midst, they said to Him,
> "Teacher, this woman has been caught in adultery, in the very
> act. Now in the Law Moses commanded us to stone such
> women; what then do You say?" And they were saying this,
> testing Him, in order that they might have grounds for accus-
> ing Him. But Jesus stooped down, and with His finger wrote
> on the ground. (John 8:1–6)

What did He write on the ground? Nobody really knows.
Some say He wrote the Ten Commandments. Others say He
wrote the seventh commandment.

The Scripture continues:

> But when they persisted in asking Him, He straightened up,
> and said to them, "He who is without sin among you, let him
> be the first to throw a stone at her." (John 8:7)

Jesus did not say the woman was not guilty. He made no
attempt to defend her actions before her pious, hypocritical

accusers. He simply said, "He who is without sin, let him cast the first stone."

They were not prepared to merely throw rocks at the adulteress. The Law said she was to be stoned to death, and they were prepared to do that. But when Jesus challenged anyone present who was not guilty to cast the first stone, one by one they departed from the scene. When confronted with the ugliness of their own sins, their shame and guilt drove them away.

If we are going to restore a brother or sister to Christ, we must come in the spirit of gentleness, humility, and love. The Scripture plainly warns, "For if anyone thinks he is something when he is nothing, he deceives himself" (Gal. 6:3). If we think we are morally or spiritually superior to the fallen brethren, not only are we badly deceived, but also we are incapable of adequately restoring others. Restoration can never take place in a cavalier atmosphere.

We still have the indwelling principle of sin within us. We are all vulnerable. That is why each of us is to "examine his own work, and then he will have reason for boasting in regard to himself alone, and not in regard to another" (Gal. 6:4).

WHEN LEADERS STUMBLE

Particularly damaging to the body of Christ is the demise of a spiritual leader, one who has visible influence before the world. When a spiritual leader falls, it is a warning signal to the nation. It is a signal for self-examination; it is a call to personal soul-searching. After all, if a man of such stature can blunder, are we too not subject to the same failures?

Tragically, however, the second signal is one of self-deception. When a prominent spiritual figure falls, it relieves pressure from unbelievers living in sin and violating the law of God.

They observe what happens and rationalize, "See there, I'm not so bad after all. This man studies the Bible and preaches to others. Look at him. If he can do that, I'm not so bad after all. What I do is no worse, and I don't even claim to be a Christian. If God loves him the way he is living, then He surely must love me too." So, temporarily, they feel some relief from the guilt or conviction they may have frequently experienced before.

It should be clear from the Scriptures that we have a Christian responsibility to restore a fallen brother or sister. It should also be clear that this sensitive, delicate issue must be handled with great care, lest we greatly damage our witness to the unbelieving world.

QUESTIONS FOR PERSONAL GROWTH

1. Identify and discuss three reasons the Bible gives for believers stumbling.

2. Despite knowing what the Bible says, believers are vulnerable to stumbling. Name seven factors that contribute to believers, taking "bites out of the forbidden fruit."

3. Identify and discuss the six principles for restoration.

4. What is your responsibility toward a fallen brother or sister?

Conclusion

Forgiveness is liberating, but it is also sometimes painful. It is liberating because we are freed from the heavy load of guilt, bitterness, and anger we have harbored within. It is painful because it is difficult to have to face ourselves, God, and others with our failures. It seems easier to blame others and go on defending our position of being right, even though we continue to hurt. But the poison of an unforgiving spirit that permeates our entire lives, separating us from God and friends, can never be adequately defended. It is devastating to our spiritual and emotional well-being and to our physical health.

Has there ever been a time in your life when you came to grips with your rebellion against God, acknowledged your need of His forgiveness, and trusted Christ as your personal Savior? Are you keeping short accounts with Him? That is, when you disobey Him, do you confess it immediately and walk on in His Spirit, enjoying your fellowship with Him?

Are you still unable to forgive someone who hurt you deeply and you still bear the scars? How long will you remain a prisoner to your own unforgiving spirit? You have within you the power to forgive, to be healed, and to be set free to live your life to the fullest.

Before you close the cover of this book, forgive the one who has hurt you even as your heavenly Father has forgiven you, and *be really free!*

Appendix A

THE UNPARDONABLE SIN

Through the years I have talked with many Christians and non-Christians who were afraid they had committed "the unpardonable sin." Just about everyone had a different understanding of exactly what that was. But they all agreed on one thing: They were guilty and felt that theirs was a hopeless situation.

Hundreds of verses in the Bible promise the forgiveness of our sins, but only one passage refers to an unforgivable sin. Let's examine the passage to gain insight into what Jesus meant when He referred to a sin that cannot be forgiven.

Jesus had healed a demon-possessed man who was blind and dumb, "so that the dumb man spoke and saw" (Matt. 12:22). The multitudes following Jesus began to say, "This man cannot be the Son of David, can he?" (v. 23). The implication was that they believed He was the Son of David, in other words, the Messiah.

On the other hand, the Pharisees accused Jesus of casting out demons by Beelzebub, the ruler of the demons. Jesus' response to their accusation was:

> Therefore I say to you, any sin and blasphemy shall be forgiven men, but blasphemy against the Spirit shall not be forgiven. And whoever shall speak a word against the Son of Man, it shall be forgiven him; but whosoever shall speak against the Holy Spirit, it shall not be forgiven him, either in this age, or in the age to come. (Matt. 12:31–32)

The term *blasphemy* may be defined "defiant irreverence." We would apply the term to such sins as cursing God or willfully degrading things considered holy. In this passage the term refers to the declaration of the Pharisees who had witnessed undeniable evidence that our Lord was performing miracles in the power of the Holy Spirit. Yet they attributed the miracles to Satan. In the face of irrefutable evidence they ascribed the work of the Holy Spirit to that of Satan.

I agree with a host of biblical scholars that this unique circumstance cannot be duplicated today. The Pharisees had seen proof after proof that Christ was who He claimed to be. They could not escape the fact that what He was doing was supernatural in nature. But instead of acknowledging what I believe they knew in their hearts was true, they attributed the supernatural power to that of Satan instead of the Holy Spirit. That, in a sense, was the last straw.

Christ is not in the world as He was then. Although the Holy Spirit is still accomplishing supernatural things through His servants, they are merely representatives of the King. The circumstances of Matthew 12 make it impossible for this sin to take place today. This incident, I might add, is the only one in which a sin is declared unforgivable. The Bible clearly states, "for whoever will call upon the name of the Lord will be saved" (Rom. 10:13). No invitation to salvation carries with it an exception clause, "unless you have committed the unpardonable sin."

No matter how evil our sins, there is pardon for them. God forgave David for his adultery, dishonesty, and murder (2 Sam. 12:13; Ps. 51). He forgave the prodigal for his "loose living." Simon Peter's triple denial of our Lord accompanied by profanity was forgiven (Matt. 26:74–75). The apostle Paul was forgiven of his preconversion merciless persecution of Christians (Acts 9:1).

Although there is no unpardonable sin, there is an unpardonable state—the state of unbelief. There is no pardon for a person who dies in unbelief. The Bible refers to this in terms of having a hard heart. The hardening of the heart is not a onetime act. It is the result of a gradual progression in which sin and the conviction of the Holy Spirit are ignored. Time is a major factor. Grieving the Spirit can progress to resisting the Spirit, which can progress to quenching the Spirit, which (unless there is repentance toward God) can ultimately result in the hardening of the heart against God (Heb. 3:7–8). The hardened heart has no desire for the things of God. Some interpret this to be the unpardonable sin. But if you have any desire in your heart for God, as expressed through concern that you may have committed some sort of unpardonable sin, you do not have a hardened heart.

Appendix B

STEPS TO
FORGIVING OTHERS

The following is included to facilitate personal application of Chapter 8.

1. Understand that forgiveness is not
   - justifying, understanding, or explaining why the person acted toward you as he or she did.
   - just forgetting about the offense and trusting time to take care of it.
   - asking God to forgive the person who hurt you.
   - asking God to forgive you for being angry or resentful against the person who offended you.
   - denying that you were really hurt; after all, there are others who have suffered more.
2. Understand that it is often unwise to forgive face-to-face. This tends to make the other person feel "put down" and make you look holier-than-thou.

3. Select a time and place when you can be alone for a season of time.

4. Pray and ask the Holy Spirit to bring to your mind all the people you need to forgive and the events you need to forgive them for.

5. Make a list of everything the Holy Spirit brings to your mind, even if it seems trivial to you. (Do not rush through this step; allow the Holy Spirit all the time He needs to speak to you.)

6. Take two chairs and arrange them facing each other. Seat yourself in one of the chairs.

7. Imagine that the first person on your list is sitting in the other chair. Disclose everything you can remember that the person has done to hurt you. Do not hold back the tears or the emotions that accompany the confessions.

8. *Choose by an act of your will to forgive that person once and for all time.* You may not feel like being forgiving. That's all right. Just do it and the feelings will follow. God will take care of that. Do not doubt that what you have done is real and valid.

9. Release the person from the debt you feel is owed you for the offense. Say, *"You are free and forgiven."*

10. If the person is still a part of your life, now is a good time to accept the individual without wanting to change aspects of personality or behavior.

11. Thank the Lord for using each person as a tool in your life to deepen your insight into His grace and to conform you to the image of His Son.

12. Pray. This is a suggested prayer to pray as you "talk" to each person:

> *Because I am forgiven and accepted by Christ, I can now forgive and accept you, _____, unconditionally in Christ. I choose now to forgive you, _____, no matter what you did to me. I release you from the hurts (take time to name the hurts). And you are no longer accountable to me for them. You are free.*

13. When you have finished praying through the hurts you have suffered, pray this prayer of faith:

> *Lord Jesus, by faith, I receive Your unconditional love and acceptance in the place of this hurt, and I trust you to meet all my needs. I take authority over the Enemy, and in the name of Jesus, I take back the ground I have allowed Satan to gain in my life because of my attitude toward _____. Right now I give this ground back to the Lord Jesus Christ, to whom it rightfully belongs.*

ACKNOWLEDGMENTS

I especially want to thank my son, Andy, for his help in research and editing, and my publisher, Victor Oliver, for his encouragement and assistance.

ABOUT THE AUTHOR

Charles Stanley is pastor of the 15,000-member First Baptist Church in Atlanta, Georgia, and twice has been elected president of the Southern Baptist Convention. He is well known through his IN TOUCH radio and television ministry to thousands internationally and is the author of many books, including *Walking Wisely*, *The Source of My Strength*, *Enter His Gates*, *Success God's Way*, and *Our Unmet Needs*.

Dr. Stanley received his bachelor of arts degree from the University of Richmond, his bachelor of divinity degree from Southwestern Theological Seminary, and his master's and doctor's degrees from Luther Rice Seminary.

Other Resources from Charles Stanley

Walking Wisely
Audio kit, video kit, workbook

Have you ever gone hiking and lost your way? One or two wrong turns can leave you disoriented or even totally lost. Dr. Stanley teaches that as you walk with God, His Word will serve as the compass that guides your steps and assures your safety.

Four-tape audio set with workbook
Order WWSET $29.95 (Canada $40.95)

Two-tape video set with workbook
Order VWWSET 29.95 (Canada $40.95)

Additional workbook, 64 pages
Order WWKB $8.95 (Canada 11.95)

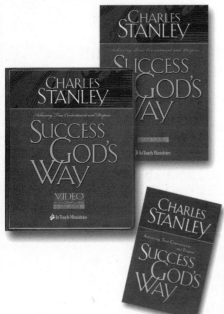

Success God's Way
Audio kit, video kit, compact disc kit, or softcover book

What is the secret to your success? Is it talent, education, or maybe leadership? These qualities are fine, but true success starts and ends with God's Word. Dr. Stanley teaches that only as we read, study, apply, and obey the Scriptures can we enjoy true and lasting success. The *Success God's Way* kit includes 10 hours of teaching plus a 200-page workbook.

Ten-CD set with workbook
Order SGWSETCD $74.95 (Canada $99.95)

Ten-tape audio set with workbook
Order SGWSET $74.95 (Canada $99.95)

Four-tape video set with workbook
Order VSGWSET $74.95 (Canada $99.95)

Softcover book, 240 pages
Order SGWBKP $14.95 (Canada $21.95)

IN TOUCH MINISTRIES® P.O. Box 7900 Atlanta, Georgia 30357
IN TOUCH MINISTRIES OF CANADA Box 4900 Markham, Ontario L3R 6G9
800-323-3747 (US and Canada)
www.intouch.org

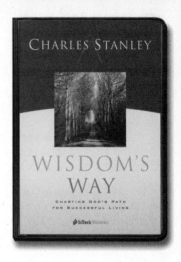
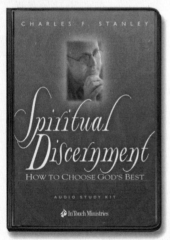